Salty Coffee

D1281580

Salty Coffee

Untold Stories by Jewish Women

Title of the Hungarian original: *Sós kávé*

Copyright © 2007 Katalin Pécsi

Novella Publishing

The publication of this book was made possible by the MAZSÖK Foundation and the Brandeis University's Hadassah International Research Institute on Jewish Women

Thanks are due to Judy Weiszenberg Cohen and Nicole Katz for their selfless work in preparing this book for publication.

Esther's Books

Collected and compiled by Katalin Pécsi
All rights reserved

ISBN 978-963-9442-88-7
ISSN 1785-4113

Novella Publishing is a member of the Association of Hungarian Book Publishers and Distributors founded in 1795.

www.novellakiado.hu

Novella Publishing
Design and cover: Dió Stúdió
Layout: B–TEX 2000 Bt.
Printed by ETO-Print Press

All rights reserved. No part of this book may be reproduced in any form or by any means, except by a reviewer who may quote brief passages in a review to be printed in a magazine or newspaper, without permission in writing from the author of the story to be quoted.

Table of Contents

Motto: *„One Jew says, just for argument's sake, because God knows a Jew loves a good argument, "Being a woman and being a Jew are two different things."*
"How so?" says the other Jew.
"One is a burden and the other is a curse."
"Oi, so true. But there is a time when the woman and the Jew becomes a Jewish woman."
"Oh," says the other one, "when is that, nu?"

Nicole Katz: Imaginary Jewish Tales

EDITOR'S FOREWORD
"UNTOLD STORIES BY JEWISH WOMEN"

The twentieth century came and went, yet hardly any recordings for posterity took place on women's living conditions, their extraordinary experiences and their multifaceted activities.

In addition, in the writings of Jewish women their Jewish identity was frequently elusive.

Why is '*the woman*' absent in Hungarian Jewish literature?

Why is being Jewish absent from the writings of Jewish women – that is, discussing, describing and analyzing issues and themes in connection to Judaism?

Women are hardly even present in Hungarian Jewish literature. Before World War Two, Hungarian women writers of Jewish origin did not identify themselves as such, and since the Holocaust, new generations of women writers have again been unwilling to write about their Jewish and/or women's identity. So the female side of the Jewish existence is absent from the general Jewish narrative. East of the Elbe gender is as problematic as ethnicity.

Why in Hungarian women's writings, aside from a few memoirs, is the Holocaust a missing theme?

For too long the Holocaust has been seen in male terms, obscuring the nature of the specific roles, work, and suffering of women. Today it seems doubly difficult to grasp what Jewish women endured, both as Jews and as women, because we don't have many memoirs or personal records written by women to draw upon.

Researchers of oral history on the Holocaust were the first ones to discover that in women's remembrances there is a different viewpoint; a different emphasis and tone came to the fore than in men's recollections. For this reason, the female perspective and narration of women's Holocaust experiences enrich and enlighten us further, and differently, even though many opportunities were lost to deepen our collective knowledge.

A painful void exists to today: not knowing the stories of the mothers, the grandmothers, the friendships in the camps, the connections, the survivors' difficult journeys home, an absence of literature and other pictorial representations, and the missing endeavors of the "second generation", the children of survivors.

In 2002, as a member of *Esztertáska, (Esther's Bag), a Jewish cultural women's group,* I made a decision to undertake the task of collecting and sharing with interested individuals as many as possible hitherto untold women's stories.

We began looking for subjective accounts of real-life stories, based on personal experiences, expressed sensitively and enhanced with details, about any and all varied aspects of their Jewish life: childhood, school, love, marriage, emigration, aliyah, resistance, hiding, assimilation and Jewish renewal after the profound political changes of 1989.

It seems we stumbled onto something that had already begun germinating. All we had to do was open the door, and suddenly we were flooded with personal histories.

It is not mere chance that these stories remained untold for so long, because as we all know it is extremely difficult to talk about life's traumatic events. A trust had to grow between the storytellers and myself. Only then was each one able to share her experiences with me, with her peers and eventually with a wider audience.

Remarkable friendships formed in this process, nurtured by mutual trust and respect, continue on today. Some of them I came to view maternally, others have said they felt similarly about me. With all the "children of the Holocaust" I've met I feel a great affinity. It is an added pleasure that a few of our non-Jewish friends also told us their stories, particularly as they pertain to Jewish people and to their Jewish friends.

The testimonies were presented at a series of readings which took place in Budapest. The first reading of untold stories, organized by the *Esztertáska* group, was held on the closing day of an exhibit called "The Jewish Woman" at the Budapest Jewish Museum, in September 2002. It was a great success, 'standing room' only, and so we decided to organize other readings, too. In the recently opened *Ráday Book Emporium;* in the newly founded *Women's House;* in the very popular *Nyitott Műhely* cultural center; in *Szimpla Kert, an "alternative" café in the heart of what was the Jewish ghetto;* and on two occasions in the Z'Art Galéria /*Retorta Kávéház* (which has since sadly closed down).

These readings had a profound effect, not only on me, but also on the audience, and likewise on the readers of our web site. In addition to organizing these readings, I became guardian of the written texts which has been an unforgettable experience, a gift in fact.

On these reading nights we usually listened to four or five authors telling their stories. In between, to ease the atmosphere and change the mood, we listened to live music: Jewish and non-Jewish folk music, world music and jazz. From one such event to the next the audience increased, by word of mouth and through personal connections. The snowball we began rolling had transformed itself into an avalanche.

Naturally, the majority of the writings are about Holocaust experiences, but well represented are also the younger, second and even third generation descendants of survivors. Among our storytellers are professional and lay writers – the latter in greater numbers. I'd rather not differentiate – these stories are not to be viewed as artistic endeavors, but rather as an honest documentation of worthy life stories.

We translated the oral stories into English and they are also now on the website in both languages. We also received several contributions from abroad: Germany, Australia, England, the US and Israel. In order not to overload this edition, a few of the stories were omitted. I trust that sooner or later they will find their proper place in a future edition.

The writings are organized thematically, which at the same time also meant that the stories more or less fell into chronological order. The stories generally begin with "happy, peaceful" times in history, followed by the fearful and threatening Holocaust era, which includes stories about ghetto life, the concentration camps, forced labor, hiding, the return and the homecoming.

The "second generation", the children of Holocaust survivors, also speak out and find their voice. As well as their non-Jewish peers who, for a variety of reasons, feel a strong connection to their Jewish friends and gravitate toward Jewish culture.

I would like to express my thanks to every single member of the *Eszter-táska Women's Group*. They, with their good advice and sense of organization, helped to arrange readings, to apply for funding and to spread our good name and to pave the way for future "Untold Women's Stories."

I am grateful to those of our friends who came to the readings and found them meaningful, and encouraged one another to write and so inspired us to continue. This book would not exist without the generous assistance of friends – *Judy Weissenberg Cohen* in Toronto, and *Nicole Katz* in Budapest – and their job-like patience in undertaking the painstaking and meticulous work of proof-reading and editing each and every story in English.

The first edition – in Hungarian – was published in April 2007. During the long years devoted to collecting these stories, some of the women have passed away: *Anna Kun, Anna Lázár, Edit Kemény and Ibolya Scheer.* Still, I dare hope the news will reach them somehow that finally their stories can also be read in a book – in Hungarian and in English, as well.

This anthology of *untold stories* is for all those who believe that the puzzle we call history is comprised of the fragments of individuals and personal stories. We hope that these *untold stories* will also resonate with the next generation, and that they may one day be used as educational tools in schools and Holocaust studies programs, to teach and inspire tolerance and acceptance.

Katalin Pécsi

Katalin Pécsi

Katalin Pécsi, Ph.D., is an essayist and a lecturer in the field of contemporary Jewish literature and film and numerous issues related to the Holocaust and Jewish women's literature. She is the director of education at the Holocaust Memorial Center in Budapest. She was a co-founder of Esther's Bag, a small but energetic, Jewish women's group in Hungary, in 2002. She is also the founder and the current chair of a new Jewish women's association, EszterHáz (Esther's House / Beth Esther) which focuses on the contemporary Jewish culture and the feminist values.

Irene Reti

DOILIES

My grandmother Margit Grunbaum, who was born in Budapest in 1900, died four years ago, at the age of 96. When she died, I inherited 25 fine lace doilies. Every arm of every chair, every table, every cabinet, in my grandmother's apartment in California had been adorned with these doilies. They are elaborate and demonstrate great skill with the crochet needle. Although I received the doilies gratefully as part of my inheritance, my feelings about them are ambivalent. For the doilies were crafted by my red-haired great-grandmother Regina, and to me they symbolize her constricted life as a woman.

I picture Regina in her apartment in Buda, her fingers nervously crocheting doilies, twisting the sadness and anxiety in her hands into permanent creations of lace, lace I hold in my own hands, across the world 100 years later. Her husband Jakab is mocking her, harshly criticizing her. Perhaps it is the Sabbath. Perhaps it is Passover. She has prepared the dinner according to his wishes but again he has found fault. She sits trembling, while he screams about a mistake she has made.

Now she is sitting rigid in the living room, the needles jerking back and forth. She wants to read, but remembers him jeering at her last night, "Again you read! My electric light costs good money." It is the early 20th century. There are no such words: battered woman, abuse.

But still she found the strength to rebel. This rebellion took a variety of forms. Sundays she snuck off to the Catholic Basilica, where leaning against a marble pillar, she felt closer to God. As a young girl my grandmother Margit accompanied her on these journeys of rebellion, in what Regina called, her double religion. Secretly she studied French, secretly because Jakab did not believe women should study. And she refused to teach her daughter how to cook and clean house. In this way she believed she would help Margit become a professional woman, and live the life she herself could not lead. When my grandmother was a teenager, she helped Regina escape on the train to Sarospatak, the town of her birth. But when they reached Sarospatak, Margit's two brothers begged her to return home, they said they could not live without her. So she returned to her home, where she dressed in the finest clothes, and made more and more doilies.

Jakab was opposed to Margit's decision to attend medical school. Because of rising anti-Semitism under Horthy, (Regent of Hungary) Margit was forced to leave Budapest and attend school in Prague. When she asked her father for tuition money he said, "A woman to be a doctor!? Go wherever you want. I will not send you a penny!" She went to Prague anyway.

She received some help from her uncle Erwin Moskowits, of Sarospatak, who was also a doctor. Still, she was very poor. My grandmother often told me how she would buy an apple and ration sections of it for each day. She was literally starving. But she was determined to be a doctor. By the time she came home to visit her parents she was emaciated. She, for once, was ashamed. Her mother kept feeding her, and whispered that her greatest wish was for her to be a doctor. This wish she inscribed on a photograph of herself which hung above my grandmother's bed.

Regina coughed through her last years, and died of tuberculosis. When Margit left Hungary in 1939 she missed Regina terribly. War made communication difficult, and my grandmother only learned of Regina's death from a Hungarian-language newspaper in Turkey.

My grandmother did become a doctor, first in Budapest, and then in Russia during the 1930s. The Holocaust propelled her out of Hungary, and into years as a refugee, first in Turkey, and then in Venezuela. Being a refugee prevented her from practicing medicine for over twenty years. But when she immigrated to the United States at age 60, my grandmother studied for her medical exams in English, my grandfather prompting her with flashcards. She once again became a doctor, and practiced medicine in the United States until she was 75.

It is the year 2000. I am visiting Budapest for the first time. I am standing by Regina's grave. "Moskowits Regina: 1878-1941," the gravestone reads. I imagine that we are studying together under a pool of electric light. I wrap my arms around the marble, imagining that I am hugging the warmth of my great-grandmother. I learn her Hebrew name: Rivka. "Rivka," I whisper, and decide to take her Hebrew name. I trace the stone tenderly, with fingers that have never crocheted doilies.

Irene Reti
Irene Reti is an oral historian, publisher and writer who lives in Santa Cruz, California. Due to the trauma they experienced during the Holocaust, her Hungarian Jewish family kept their identity a secret from her until she was seventeen. Her memoir The Keeper of Memory was published in 2001. Reti taught oral history workshops in the Bet Debora conference in 2001 and 2003 and did her master's thesis on Jewish women and memory work in post-Holocaust Europe. She is currently working on a historical novel about gender and kabbalah that takes place during the expulsion of the Jews from Iberia in 1492.

Ibolya Scheer

"TZEDOKO TATZIL MIMOVES" OR "CHARITY DRIVES DEATH AWAY"

I know, some will say: Oh dear, Ibolya is going to tell tales about her childhood again! I don't refute this and as you had all been children, you all very well know that these experiences last long, they also influence the formation of our character. Many people cannot or will not remember. I'm not one of them. I can and I will. And it relieves me to tell you about my memories. So there you go:

I was 8 years old in 1934. I was skinny and small. My whole family lived in the 7th district of Budapest. My grandfather, a grey-bearded, clever orthodox Jew had a restaurant in Wesselényi street. He taught me to read Hebrew, taught me the magnificence of theJewish religion and knowledge, the meaning of the Ten Commandments and the secrets and mysteries of the Torah. He always started the daily lessons after his afternoon nap. The room next to the restaurant was full of old books treasuring wisdom and learning. My chassid grandfather, well-versed in the mysteries of Rashi, Maimonides, Rambam, the Talmud and the Kabbalah shared his light afternoon meal with me. That was a time of asking questions. – Come, Sorele – he would say – it's time to learn. – And he taught me kindly, cleverly, with patience. Once I complained to him about how hard it was for me to carry those 10-12 packs made by my grandmother for the poor in the neighbourhood with the barches, the meat and fish, a little wine and some cake. – Sorele! – my grandfather would say. – If it was easy, it wouldn't be such a great MITZVAH for you. TZEDOKO TATZIL MIMOVES! – charity drives death away. For a Jew – he went on – the greatest mitzvah is charity. To help those in need is a deed pleasing to the Lord. – So this was how he taught me the morals and rules of religion far from being easy.

He was often asked: Listen, mister! What d'you teach this little girl for? You have some 20 grand-sons!

– This little girl read Hebrew texts at the age of 4! It's time she understood now what she's reading! – he answered.

We had a great time studying together. He had a great sense of humour. I loved him. I sat into the armchair and took the heavy book in my lap. I was reading and he explained me everything patiently. When I made a mistake, he corrected me kindly. This peaceful process of learning went on until I got 12 years old, when I had pupils myself. But let's get back to '34.

My mother – who was a Weisz girl – only laughed at his father who picked this snotty little one, me, as a pupil. Mother only knew the practical side of religion. The rules of kosher, of Sabbath and the rythm of feasts, but the causes and the question *why* simply left her untouched. I, on the opposite, was interested in all these. I loved and admired my mother. She brought up her children (four girls and a boy) and looked after them with selfless devotion. I respected her honesty, her efficiency, her strength and common sense. She kept our shop (kosher poultry) as clean as her home. She was a great housewife. She sew all our clothes herself.

The autumn feasts were approaching. Mother sew us four identical dresses. She asked old Mr. Müller in Akácfa street to make us four pairs of patent-leather shoes with cream-coloured insert. It cost altogether 12 Pengős which equalled the price of two full geese. The dresses and the shoes were all prepared in time and my father decided to have his four "beautiful" daughters photographed by photographer Sontag in Király street the following day. In brand new dresses and brand new shoes – he said – standing next to one another just like pipes of the organ.

On a September day, a little before Rosh Hashanah as I came home from elementary school, I found my mother in a state of dreadful agony, moaning and writhing with pain. I'd never seen such agony before. I got very frightened and stood nailed to the ground. Then screaming I ran for my father to the shop. I could hardly stammer out what happened at home. He phoned Dr. Appel right away, closed the shop and we were headed for home. My mother could barely speak then. The doctor came in a hurry and gave her a Papaverin shot. – That's a bilious attack – he declared and gave her some instructions. – You lie down, Mrs. Scheer and rest and stay away from working if you want to avoid operation! – I was still horrified and trembled like a leaf as a result of the awful shock I'd gone through. I was afraid my mother would die. Oh, my God, what am I to do? Then I suddenly remembered my wise old grandfather's teaching which I believed firmly: "Charity drives death away." Now I'm going to drive death away! I wrapped up my beautiful new pair of shoes and went down to Klauzál square. I picked a little girl out of many who only had worn sandals on her feet and had more patches than clothes. I gave her my lovely shoes and ran. And came home with peace in my heart. Tzedoko tatzil mimoves. I secretly believed my mother was healed by the Lord in the meantime. Unfortunately she still lay in bed white as wax. I couldn't understand it at all. After all I have done the mitzvah pleasing to the Lord!

Apparently, I thought, this was not enough for the Lord. So, I took the shoes of my six-year-old sister Magdi and went back to the square. I picked another little girl with worn sandals and gave them these shoes. Then I stormed back home wondering what I would find. Mum got a little better thanks to the antispasmodic. If only slowly, she started pacing up and down the room. I was beside myself with joy because I was absolutely convinced she got better owing to my tzedok requiring great self-sacrifice. God at last acknowledged and accepted my good deed. He drove the angel of death away from my mother. Father, however, only glared at me when I told him proudly, with shining eyes what I'd done for mother. Where those lovely new shoes had gone. My little sister wept, my father was speechless. He thought for a moment he was imagining things.

– Rózsi! – he called to my mother. – Rózsi, is this girl daft or what? Has Ibolya gone totally crazy? That pair of shoes cost me 3 Pengős!

He was mad. I cried like a baby. I locked myself up into the bathroom in my grief. Even my own mother failed to understand me! No one understood me!

We had our photos taken the following day, my little sister and I had white canvas shoes on, Edit and Éva had the new ones. Sadness shows on my face. I still have this photo. Mr. Müller, the shoe-maker could make new shows for us only for Yom Kippur to make up for the "tzedoke" ones. That's how I became known as "Ibolya the Impostor" at home. Only my beloved grandfather's expression revealed that he believed me my mother had been cured by the help of the Lord as I could drive the angel of death away.

I will never forget this true story. I remember it each year at Rosh Hashanah. That's a real true story. Believe me! Look here, I show you the picture! To tell lies in the name of great names is a sin, this what my dear, beloved grandfather, Mendel Weisz would say.

Translation by Ágnes Merényi

Ibolya Scheer
Ibolya Scheer and her three sisters grew up in a Chasidic family. She went to Dob Utca Orthodox Elementary School. When she was 12 years old she joined Hashomer Hatzair, a left-wing Zionist youth group. Later she became a communist, and was arrested soon after the German occupation. For a while she shared a prison cell with Hannah Szenes. She was then deported to concentration camp. After the war she went to art school but as she had to provide for her family she felt she couldn't become an artist. She finished high school at the age of 40 when her children were already grown up and then she obtained a university degree graduating with distinction. In retirement she was an active member of WIZO and MAZSIKE (Hungarian Jewish Cultural Association). Over the last few years she has begun to tell many of her untold stories, especially to the younger generations. In 2006 Ibolya Scheer passed away.

Ibolya Scheer

CHANUKAH CANDLES IN THE KITCHEN WINDOW

It is the custom in Jewish families that on Chanukah when the candles are lit the menorah is placed in a window facing the street, so that all the world can witness the holiness and beauty of the festival flames. My father, being a religious man, always followed this custom. However, on three separate occasions, during the many decades of his life, I saw my father light the Chanukah candles in the kitchen window. Each occasion tells a different story, each with its very own reasons. I hope you'll enjoy these stories about Chanukah candles, kitchens and holy flames.

1.

My parents owned a general store at 23 Wesselényi utca. They sold kosher poultry, fruit and vegetables. We lived nearby, at 12 Nagydiófa utca, in a huge apartment building. It had a large courtyard with many small apartments and countless kids. There was a common well and one toilet for every floor. Our apartment had two rooms overlooking the street and all in all was quite comfortable. We lived close to the Kazinczy utca synagogue, the school and the store.

My father used to go out to the market in Csepel at three or four in the morning to buy fruit and vegetables for the shop. One a summer day a street porter approached him and offered to sell him a tricycle for transporting goods. Up until then my father had been using a carriage, but it would be much easier and faster to carry the goods to the shop on a tricycle. As the asking price was really very low, my father decided to buy it.

This happened in 1936. I often went with him on the days when I didn't have to go to school. I enjoyed watching the bustle of the market and loved the smell of the fruit so I didn't mind getting up before dawn. I would sit proudly on the tricycle minding the goods while my father continued looking for things he needed. On the way back I sat on top of the boxes of fruit while my father pedaled, and by seven we arrived at the store with our sweet-smelling, fresh produce. I helped my parents arrange things in the shop window, so that my mother could start selling. Then my father took me by the hand and we walked home together. Éva, my older sister, made breakfast while my father washed himself in preparation for morning prayers. He took out his *tallit* and *tefillin* and turned towards the wall to pray. I also said my morning prayers. Afterwards we'd have a big breakfast, then I went to play, and he went back to the store to help my mother. They'd come home late, after eight in the evening, and they only ever rested on the Sabbath. They worked hard for little money and had many debtors.

One day, just as we were just unloading the goods from the tricycle, a man came up to my father and said:

"That's my tricycle. I recognize it. You stole it from me!" My father was shocked.

"I did not steal it, I bought it from a porter," he said. He even knew the porter's number, which they used to wear on their caps, but to no avail. The man reported him to the police. My father had unwittingly become the receiver of stolen goods.

Four months later the trial took place. It fell on the eighth day of Chanukah. I asked my father to let me accompany him as I was curious to see what a trial was like. I will never forget it. The porter admitted that he'd stolen the tricycle and sold it to my father. The judge asked my father:

"Mr. Scheer, didn't you suspect that the tricycle was so cheap because it was stolen?!"

"But your honor," he said, "I bought it in broad daylight!" Everyone present burst out laughing. My father was so ashamed. He thought that crimes could only be committed after dark. The judge imposed a heavy fine on him, he had to pay 100 pengos and the tricycle was confiscated. 100 pengos meant a lot in 1936! It was already getting dark when we arrived back at the store. We were left empty-handed. We were sad. My father was ashamed of being involved in such a nasty court case. He, who was such an honest, deeply religious Jew. How could he go home now to light the holy candles? We trudged home sadly.

We'd moved into a new apartment a few months before. At the time my father didn't realize that the windows of our two rooms looked onto a brothel. The prostitutes slept during the day, and at night the tavern under our apartment was their regular haunt. As we approached they began hurling obscenities at my father. He didn't answer them, he just headed for the front gate and dragging me along behind him. Once in the courtyard he was overcome with anger and disgust. How would he be able to celebrate Chanukah in this state of mind! The ugly court case, the heckling prostitutes, it was all too much for him. He couldn't eat dinner, even though my mother had made sweet latkes and baked pumpkin for the holiday.

After being at home with us a while he calmed down. He went into his room to prepare the menorah. He put the eight colorful candles in, and then added the ninth one, the *shames*, the one that would light all the others. He was about to call us in when he heard the raucous laughter of the prostitutes leaving the tavern. So he took the menorah, brought it out to the kitchen and put it in the window which overlooked the courtyard. Away from the drunken laughter he lit the candles, and from the kitchen window they illuminated the night as we sang the *Maoz Tzur*. It was a sad Chanukah that winter, and many people believed that that year the Scheers did not light the candles.

We moved in the spring. We went to live at 11 Wesselényi utca. My father bought a new tricycle from Velvart, the city's biggest bicycle shop, and this time he asked for a receipt.

2.

My second story is about Chanukah night in 1945. It was our first Chanukah since the war had ended, we were finally free. The Scheer sisters had all made it home from the concentration camps. Auschwitz, Bergen-Belzen and Rawensbrück could not get the better of us. My younger sister had arrived home too. She'd been hiding in Pest with false identification papers. It took enormous persistence, toughness and faith to find our way back home. My parents knew that we were alive, as we'd managed to send messages, but we did not know what was awaiting us in Pest. I was the first to arrive in July. I'd been taken away from our home at 27 Dob utca, so I went back there but couldn't find anyone. I was crying. A woman came up to me:

"You're one of the Scheer girls, aren't you?"

"Yes I am" I said. "Do you know anything about my parents?"

"They survived and so have your grandparents. And their restaurant is still in one piece."

I ran down Kazinczy utca, and there on the corner of Wesselényi utca was Mendel Weisz's glatt kosher restaurant! My father was standing in the doorway. I ran into his arms. I had arrived! There were kisses, hugs and tears. My father told me how they'd survived the Shoah in the ghetto with my younger brother who was 13 and my grandparents who were in their 80s. My sisters, Éva and Edit, were still in a hospital in Germany, but they were alive and coming home soon! We were a lucky family. We were alive.

My parents had managed to get a four room apartment soon after the city had been liberated by the Russians. It was called the Civil Servants' Settlement, I'd never heard of it before, but it was to be our new home. My mother had dug up the neglected garden and planted vegetables and flowers. My father found it difficult to live there as the synagogue was very far away. The closest synagogue was next to Teleki Square which was not very close at all, and neither was the butcher or the mikveh. Still my father walked all the way back to the Kazinczy utca synagogue on Friday nights and Saturday mornings to pray. "This is not a proper place for religious Jews to live," he said about our new home, but at least his daughters had their own rooms. It was a huge sacrifice for our parents!

Our boyfriends had all been taken away to forced labor camp and survived and were waiting for us when we arrived home. In September and October that year we all got married and moved out with our husbands.

Then December came, a new Chanukah, with the whole family together again at last, only now there were even more of us! Miklós, Karcsi, Jeno, Pista my brother, the three sisters my parents and grandparents, we made a nice big family.

My father tried to get Chanukah candles in Pest. Now we needed 44 candles, but there weren't any, not even Christmas tree candles. He couldn't even get oil wicks. There were no candles anywhere. I decided to go to the corner grocery store. The owner, Mr. Barta, could get anything for hard currency, so I asked him if he could get candles for me.

"Well, maybe, I've got twenty altar candles for the parson on Rezso Square. I found them in my village. They were left over from before the war. Will they do for you?" "Of course," I answered, but I had no idea what they looked like. He took out two of the tapers, they were one meter long and an inch wide. Of course I didn't tell him what I needed them for, but I paid five dollars for them. I brought my spoils home. I found some embroidering thread, reheated the candles in a pot in the laundry and re-moulded them into 44 Chanukah candles. I hung them up on a string to dry and later I painted them with distemper. I liked them. I waited for my father to come home from the store. It was winter, and it was getting dark early. After supper I gave him the candles. "Look, Papa, we can still light the candles. I made these myself," I told him. He was not really interested in how I'd managed to get them. For him it was natural, if God wants him to light candles, he will provide. That's the way it was.

My father took out the beautiful menorah they'd managed to save. He put the candles in, I could tell he didn't really like them, but they were all we had. He took the menorah straight into the kitchen which overlooked the garden and lit them there. He called us all together. He said the blessing and then we sang *Maoz Tzur*. It was our first religious holiday together since the war. My father blessed us, and gave thanks to God for saving us all. We wept at the sound of our song. We were a rare family after the Holocaust. Later I asked my father why he had lit the candles in the kitchen window and not in the front room. He said that it was a strange neighborhood, not our world and none of anyone's business what we did. He said that God heard our prayers and songs and saw the light from the kitchen window too.

Soon after they moved to 18 Wesselényi Utca. There they could light the Chanukah candles in the front room, and the synagogue was much closer too so it was easy for them to walk there. And well, the parson only got 18 candles, as Mr. Barta told him that was all he had. But surely those 18 candles must have been enough for Jesus, after all, he was also a nice Jewish boy.

3.

The third story happened much later, in 1970, in Israel. My parents moved to Israel in 1950. My younger brother had already been studying there. My grandfather was 90, and my grandmother was 86 when they left Hungary. My uncle was waiting for them. He'd arranged a cosy new home for my grandparents, who both died there in 1958. After living together for 80 years in a loving marriage they could not go on living without one another.

My father was 58 and my mother 53 when they made *aliyah*, nevertheless they found the strength to build new lives for themselves. They built a house with a garden in the hills of Tiberias. Eli, my younger brother, Riemonte, his wife, and seven children lived in a five room apartment built on top of the house. My father sold eggs and poultry in the market. It was enough for the two of them. Eli and Riemonte lived on their teachers' wages. My mother looked after her seven little sabra grandchildren and tended the garden. She had plenty to do, but as I saw it, they were satisfied and happy.

In 1970 I came to visit them for three weeks. My parents were waiting for me at the airport. My father was 78, and my mother was 73. I was so moved when I saw them waving, I kissed them over and over again. It was after dark when we arrived to Tiberias, the city and the shimmering lake were brilliantly illuminated.

A few days later Chanukah arrived. In the afternoon my father took out his siddur and began to pray. I sat down in front of him and rudely interrupted his prayers.

"Papa, do you really think that God knows that there is an old Jew up in Tiberias who adores him and prays to him three times a day? Do you think that God has enough antennas to be able to listen to everybody's prayer?"

"What a silly girl you are, my dear," he said, his voice filled with pity and anger, "don't you know that God has angels who listen to prayers?"

"Sorry, Papa," I said, trying to calm him. "I didn't mean to interrupt your prayers or shake your faith."

"You would not be able to. You would not be able to." He repeated and went on praying, silently and devoutly.

I wished I had his faith. What a peaceful man he was, I thought. I felt ashamed. In that moment I understood the depth and greatness of his soul.

My mother was preparing the festive dinner. After his prayers, my father brought out the menorah and prepared the candles. The candles were beautiful, of course. Then he took the menorah into the kitchen and put it in the window sill. In his Israeli house it was the kitchen window that looked out onto the street. My father lit the candles, and their light was seen from as far away as the snowy peaks of Mount Hermon. That night Lake Tiberias glittered with thousands of Chanukah candles. After the blessing, the children sang *Maoz Tzur* loudly and happily. I hadn't celebrated such an intimate, special Chanukah in years.

I hope you enjoyed these stories about my father, Sraga Scheer, who died when he was 89. His grave, beside my mother's, lie in a cemetery on a windswept hill overlooking Tiberias. They were happy as their dreams were fulfilled. With the help of God I will travel back to Israel and put stones on their graves. May my parents, Sraga and Rachel Scheer rest in peace.

Translation by Bea Sándor

Ibolya Sheer

THE SIXTEENTH PRISONER

A true story. It happened eons ago.

I met Hanna Szenes in early September 1944.

Who was she? What did she mean to me?

To understand the connection between us, first I have to introduce myself, to give you the context of where we both came from – how our lives converged – for two brief months only.

I was born into an Orthodox Jewish family, on April 26, 1926. We were five siblings and we lived in Budapest, at 27 *Dob* Street. I attended the Orthodox Jewish middle school at 35 Dob Street.

When I was thirteen, my parents were planning to make Aliah, to emigrate to Palestine, but with five children, to start a new life, would have been daunting.

At that point in my life, I became a member in the left-leaning Zionist organization, *Hashomer Hatzair* and where I usually enjoyed myself. My parents would have preferred me to join *Mizrachi*, the Orthodox Jewish youth group. No matter, eventually the prevailing Fascist regime closed both of them.

I would have loved to continue with my schooling after finishing middle school but we were poor and I needed to learn a trade. I managed to start apprenticing as a dressmaker in a good Salon. My mother arranged that I didn't have to work on Shabbat. About 30 to 40 women worked in this salon, all of them trade union members. Obviously, I wanted to follow suit.

The union office was located on *Almassy Square*. I joined up and I learned a great deal from the members there. My open mind and receptive intellect soaked up what was offered around me: I learned about the importance of books, music and to be cultured. Here is where I came to understand the value of friendship, mutual help, and solidarity. These moral values were not exactly new to me. After all, my religious upbringing at home and especially what I learned from my Chasidic grandfather, *Mendel Weisz* neatly coexisted with the union values – at least, in some respects. The atheist world view was strange for me. To deny the existence of God is a "neveire", a sin for me. I debated this issue endlessly. I would not succumb to giving up my deeply felt faith. "It's all right, little girl", the union leader would intervene, "after all, religion is your private matter" and the issue was never raised again.

Observing the deepening fascism in Hungary by the enactment of more and more anti-Jewish laws and edicts convinced me that I must do something about it.

In the union there was such a possibility. In 1943, I aimed to attend the demonstration on March 15, a national, patriotic holiday, at the statue of *Sandor Petofi,* (well loved national, historical hero) and indeed I did.

By then, there was in Budapest an active anti-Fascist movement, mainly in the Iron, Leather and Tailors' unions and in the so-called *Peace* Party. Unfortunately, many of the comrades were arrested. In spite of my youth, I was seventeen and a half years old; I connected with a few of these groups. I became active and was entrusted with a number of assignments, which I carried out faithfully.

The occupation of Hungary by the Nazis, on March 19, 1944, profoundly changed my life – I became "illegal".

I saw I had no choice but to become a housemaid and found employment at *Vigado* Square 2, which included a small room of my own. From here I conducted my illegal activities: distributed leaflets; attended clandestine meetings where I received my instructions for our next action. This also gave me the opportunity to obtain documents like "officially" stamped furlough permits, food vouchers, military ID booklets for the

Yeshiva students, transferred nationals from Slovakia, in order to avoid conscription into the forced labor battalions.

Who knows what happened to them?

In April 1944, Mira Deutch gave me the mimeograph machine, once used by the Orthodox community.

With this machine it was possible for us to make leaflets, for May 1st, with the slogan:

Hungarian Workers Don't Work for the German Fascists.

Death to the German Occupiers. It felt so good.

However, it didn't last long. We were betrayed. On May 3rd, along with a number of my comrades I was arrested. For interrogation we were taken to the Gestapo office, in the *Mirabel* Hotel, located on *Svab* Hill. During seven weeks of questioning and maltreatment I confessed nothing nor did I betray my comrades. I pretended to be an innocent, ignorant and naïve young girl. A while later they closed the case, or so it seemed.

But they transferred us to the Defense Department, located on *Csillag* Hill, on *Fo* Street no.6. This was where the company of the dreaded and brutal gendarmerie (the paramilitary police) functioned. The beating, clubbing and various abusive measures started all over again. Approximately, three hundred people were subjected to and kept under inhuman conditions. The sadistic gendarmes still couldn't break me. Then the authorities closed the files of the case, again.

However, totally illegally – not allowing even the officially appointed defense lawyer to communicate with us – a military tribunal sentenced me to four years in prison – at the same time I turned 18, and was now considered an adult. Those who received the final sentencing were transferred, yet again, this time to the prison on *Conti* Street. So was I. I was locked into cell no II. 232, already occupied by 14 girls, a previously sentenced, closely-knit group. I was the 15th and the 16th bunk was empty. This was a very interesting group, made up of Hungarian communists, Serbian, Croat, Slovenian partisans, resisters and Soviet parachutists. I still remember the names of some of them. The Hungarian girls: Vera, Lici, Iren, Marta, Erzsi and me. The Serbs: Dragica, Milica, Deszanka, Jugovica, Zorka and Babaroza. Mara was a Croat. She was everyone's interpreter. The two Soviet girls, Tamara and Masa spoke four languages. It was a good *collective.* I quickly integrated into the group. They even permitted me to participate in their study sessions led by the highly educated Lici and Vera.

We kept the cell very clean. Fifteen people in a small cell must keep good order. There were debates but never arguments even though all social strata were represented there – from the old farm woman to the highly educated, and knowledgeable Hungarian communist girls and anything in between. The girls while speaking many languages and believing in different ideas were connected by their hatred for Nazism, Fascism and anger about their degradation and humiliation.

The 16th bunk was still empty.

Early in September 1944, on a balmy autumn morning, the heavy door of our cell opened and in walked the 16th prisoner.

A girl. Suddenly it got brighter. The sun shone through the small cell window and the sunlight enveloped the new girl. We fell silent – the heavy cell door was closed with a rather loud bang behind her. She looked around with a smile and shined as she said, "I am Hanna Szenes, a British officer in the volunteer Palestinian Brigade and I am Jewish." We eagerly gathered around and questioned her but she would say nothing more. She made herself at home on the straw mattress, took off her khaki jacket and took out a few personal items from a small bag. We could tell from the way she looked around with her alert eyes, she was assessing the situation she was in.

She wasn't exactly a beauty but she had two clever, luminous eyes that lit up her face. She had a Greek nose, strong chin and wore her hair in a Greek style.

She wasn't slim either. She had rather wide hips and the heavy military boots didn't flatter her legs. Still, she absolutely shined. One could not ignore her. In one hour she became the sole focus of our attention. In the beginning, she spoke infrequently but observed everything. Her comments were thoughtful and intelligent. My bunk was next to hers and I could easily observe her. She had an engaging manner.

With her clever but pointed questions it became clear to Hanna the kind of company she was surrounded by. In a few days she adjusted and became one of us. She pitched in with the cleaning and all the other work we had to do. When she saw the kind of instruction and studying that was conducted in our cell, she asked if she could share her expertise and knowledge with us – her sophisticated, worldly and military knowledge. She was well informed on a vast array of literature and her lectures were most welcome. She spoke six languages beside English. Hanna seemed to like us and she was never condescending. She taught us English, war maneuvers; grenade throwing; and rope climbing. The Serb and Croat girls admired her. She sang partisan songs with them. She learnt those songs in the Balkan Mountains while living with the partisans for a few months, waiting to be parachuted into Budapest. Her mistrust disappeared as soon as she realized that four of the five Hungarian girls were

Jewish. Only Erzsi wasn't. She was the daughter of an ironworker at the *Csepel* manufacturing company. Erzsi was a very loyal communist. Hanna was thrown together with a group of highly committed anti-Fascist young women.

Little by little she loosened up. We learned that her father was Bela Szenes a well-respected newspaper writer, who died before she made Aliah. Her mother was alive, lived in Budapest and Hanna last seen her on *Gyorskocsi* Street. She worried a lot about her mother. She talked about how she'd emigrated to Israel and lived on a kibbutz near *Cesaria*. We heard a lot about kibbutz life and the girls just lapped it up.

She said she worked and studied a great deal during the day, but at night while singing and dancing around the campfire she would get re-energized. She went through military training also and when WWII broke out she enlisted in the British army. As an officer she had been on various assignments. She volunteered for this mission too with three other comrades.

Her task was, to reach Hungary, make connections with the anti-Fascist resistance and help develop it further. In addition, she was to help in rescuing the Jewish population.*

The arrival wasn't successful. They landed, as far as I know, near *Pecs* (a city in Western Hungary) and one of her comrades was injured. People in the village noticed what happened and typically reported to the gendarmes that there were "British spies in the village." This is how she was captured and ended up in jail.

They interrogated her at the Secret Services Section. Hanna was not considered a war prisoner but a spy. She was tortured. She didn't confess though. She didn't betray her comrades even though her mother, *Katharine Szenes*, was blackmailed.

Hanna stood by her vow.

We learnt all this later from the clerk in the jail's library who read out the documents. This clerk also informed us that *Ferenc Szalasi* (the Hun-

* According to further research, Hanna's mission in Hungary, first and foremost, was to rescue British pilots, the rescue of Hungarian Jews was secondary.

garian Fascist leader) had taken over the government in October 1944 and that the Soviet army was getting close to Budapest.

In the evenings Hanna would recite poems she'd written by heart.

She was a poet too. She also kept a diary. She took it with her on November 6. I wonder who found it? With her sunny personality, her kindness and unshakable faith she was a wonderful role model. Her presence had a great influence on us. She was especially good with people, a rarity I haven't seen since.

She and I had frequent discussions, after the lights were turned off. She noticed that I didn't eat the bacon sent from the Balkans to the Serb girls. She didn't eat it either – for it was *treif*, (not kosher). She truly understood me and became my role model. I regarded her as a sister. She was everybody's favorite. Her good name spread throughout the prison, for her goodness, strength and practical skills were much admired. She was simply magnificent, and entirely modest.

In mid October 1944, my parents came to visit me. When my father saw me in my in prison garb, he said "Oh my child *reboine shelailom* if only *They* would see this misery in the heavens!" My Mother, with yellow star sewn on her jacket, was crying. They brought me food, whatever they could and enough for all 16 girls. When I asked the girls what my mother should bring us next time, Hanna laughingly declared "potato dumplings." I told my parents, adding "but bring enough for all of us." My Father visited me in November and brought an enormous pot full of still warm potato dumplings and said, "Tell that Jerusalemite girl to eat up, I brought it with love." And so it was. We ate the festive dumplings, covered in breadcrumbs – not knowing this was to be our last day together – we laughed a lot and were ebullient. It struck us as hilarious that the women at 27 *Dob* Street had prepared this huge amount of hand-made dumplings for us poor prisoners. They tasted wonderful.

The next day, on November 6, 1944, the heavy cell door opened. The keys turning in the lock sounded frightening.

Two prison guards entered calling out her name *Anna Szenes.* They gathered up all her belongings and put handcuffs on her. We were shocked. What did it mean to be transferred to the *Margit* Avenue jail to stand trial there? We sensed danger: *Szalasi*! Martial law! Kangaroo court! I was devastated. I feared for my dear Hanna, my sister. We embraced. Her handcuffs rattled. We all cried and kissed. Hanna didn't cry but her eyes were full of tears as she embraced me saying: "My little sister be courageous and strong. Tell your family and the people how all this came about, what and why it happened."

She kissed my forehead and left. Two guards surrounded her as she walked the length of the corridor with the sound of her steps echoing for a long time.

The fifteen of us didn't sleep all night. We missed Hanna. Nobody was telling magic stories about life on a kibbutz.

The following morning, on November 7, 1944, the usually talkative guy who brought our food, silently handed it in through the small cell-door window. At the dinner distribution we learned that Hanna Szenes, this sparkling star, was sentenced to die by the kangaroo court and three hours later executed in the jail yard. She courageously refused the blindfold – she died as she lived – a hero.

We were unable to eat. We mourned her as Jews mourn a sister, sitting on the floor. All day, on November 8, we continued to mourn and remained inconsolable. We wept.

On November 9, the whole building was evacuated. They deported all of us, Jews and non-Jews alike, about two hundred political prisoners, to Nazi concentration camps in Germany.

On May 3rd 1945 we were liberated, and in early July I arrived home. My entire family survived the horrors. In September, the same year, I married a most wonderful man.

In 1947 my son, and in 1949 my daughter was born. I named her *Anna,* in honor of Hanna's memory.

Ever since then, every November 7th, I light a memorial candle, to mourn and remember her.

I lived up to her request and talk about her life and her death – Hanna Szenes of blessed memory.

Translation by Judy Weiszenberg Cohen

Judit Fenákel

TO STEAL OR NOT TO STEAL

Thou shall not steal! It is one of *The Ten Commandments*.
In our circle, these *Commandments* were adhered to in earnest.
In the Catholic public school, where I learned reading and writing, it would occur, from time to time, that an underprivileged child would crave to have a school-bench classmate's eraser, sandwich or colored pencils. If caught, each time the full power of the prevailing morality descended upon the poor culprit.

In the home of my Grandma, strict about her 'old-fashioned' moral convictions: "Thou Shall Not Steal" was on an equal footing with "Thou Shall Not Kill". Therefore, till 1944, I couldn't imagine any situation where I would take another person's possessions, be that a pencil, or a slice of bread with jam, or even help myself to fruit from a tree on a street.

However, in 1944, (after the German Nazis occupied Hungary) everything changed, seemingly even the *Ten Commandments*. Because to seize other people's houses, stores, jewelry and even coffee mugs, by previously considered decent citizens, was not necessarily considered a sin.

(Of course, I am not privy to how these daily, brazen thieveries were accounted for on Sundays at the confessional.)

It is also true that by then, *Thou Shall Not Kill* also lost its moral constraint. In wars, to kill is praiseworthy, rewarded by medals. Special attention was devoted to carving-up unarmed civilians, burying alive, starving to death, or murdering people by gassing. Topsy-turvy went the entire *Ten Commandments*: sin became virtue, virtue morphed into treason.

I envy not the confessional priests whose task it was to mete out penitence to the faithful, in these confusing, turbulent situations.

The relativity of moral behavior didn't spare the victims either. Stealing in the concentration camps for example wasn't just a daredevil act but a life-saving one. For example, if one didn't manage to steal sterile bandages from the medical lab, the gaping wound on one's back, caused by the guard's whipping, would get infected and death would result from blood poisoning.

However, even if one managed to avert blood poisoning, the other possibilities one had to be wary of were: being hanged; starvation and/or freezing to death; typhus epidemic; being whipped; shot to death; medical experiments; forced marching; the minefields; and to be gassed – best to stop here.

In other words, stealing was a necessity, a must.

This was true even in our more tolerable labor camp where there was no gas chamber or forced marches. In addition there really was something to steal.

On the estate of the *Dreher* beer manufacturers the main vegetable crop was sugar beets. This clearly explains that our main food source, beside the officially requisitioned yellow pea, was sugar beet. We ate it baked, as molasses, as fake 'chestnut puree' and even as dessert. The adults stole them mainly in the evenings, and hid them in the pockets of *Juliska's* leather coat. *Juliska* was my mother's close girlfriend. They had a strong bond in good and adverse times, even in thievery. They both used, alternatively, that leather coat, which *Juliska* loaned even to strangers, meaning to those who didn't hail from *Endrod*. This particular coat was different from all the other coats because of its very deep pockets in which one could effectively hide the stolen goods without anybody noticing them. To remain undetected while stealing a great number of sugar beets was a virtue, being the best thief was both envied and revered by the camp's inmates.

We, the children, tried to emulate the grown-ups in thieving, but of course without wearing *that* leather coat. Adult-size garments wouldn't protect us – we would be all the more conspicuous. Even among us children, there were those with a great talent for walking by the guard with pockets full of stolen goods and the most innocent look on their faces. Sadly, I wasn't among those. Each time I went stealing, I had disproportionate pangs of conscience and a fear of being discovered, while the meager end result didn't make up for the anxiety I experienced.

One very ordinary day we went to steal tomatoes. Tomato were a rare delicacy. They reared their pretty red heads in a special fenced off vegetable garden. To get hold of some of them was no mean task but we pulled it off. We put them in our pockets, that is, those who had any.

I gathered these rare treasures in my skirt, which I managed to pull up and fashion into a deep pocket – then we ran like hell.

There were five of us children running toward the stables. Four managed to reach our compound without any mishap. I, on the other hand, exactly in front of the castle, stumbled, and let go of my gathered-up skirt holding the tomatoes – those small, firm tomatoes rolling all over the place in front of the cow-hand and the Dutchman who was a large, very light blond, young man, whose service rank we couldn't ascertain. We looked upon him as the assistant manager. Even today I have this adverse reaction when I am frightened , I don't run as most people would but rather, I freeze, I am numb, unable to move, just like on *that* day. I stood there, in a circle of tomatoes, motionless, afraid even to breath. I felt a knot in my stomach – my end is here! For this, beating, confinement and death will be waiting for me. One of those punishments was just as possible as the other. I knew, by then, that to us, anything could happen.

The Dutchman, on the other hand, this blond athlete with a melodic laughter, didn't pay any attention to me or to the rolling tomatoes. He absentmindedly turned around, continued to speak to the cow hand without interrupting what he was talking about – and I, with my empty skirt, hanging my head low, quietly snuck away.

Because *this* was possible, I am here.

Tranlation by Judy Weiszenberg Cohen

Judit Fenákel
Judit Fenákel was born in Budapest in 1936. She earned her Diploma of Education in Szeged University and taught in elementary school for many years before becoming a journalist. She published her first book in 1960 and since then has regularly published her short stories and novels. Her latest publications include: A Fénykép Hátoldala (Novella 2000), Hajtogatós with Ágnes Gergely (Novella 2004) and A Kékezüst Hölgy (Novella 2005).

Magda Sommer

STATIONS
(Excerpts)

...Weeks, months passed and from September on the weather turned very cold. We suffered more and more from cold, from hunger and thirst.

We became thinner and thinner.

This time, towards the end of October 1944, with the advance of the Russian army, evacuation of the camps began.

The evacuation was accompanied by "selections". (the process by which the Nazis chose who would live and who would die by gassing.)

Klári and I got selected into a labour transport with five hundred other people. We were taken to camp "A" next to our camp "C".

At the morning Zählappel (roll-call) it turned out that we were more than the required five hundred because some people, who originally were not selected for work, escaped from their barracks to this labour-block. This labour barrack was even better guarded by the SS than the others, because it was well known we were off to a work camp and a lot of people tried to join our group.

Since we were rather helpless, the others managed to push Klári and me to the far end of the line. Those at the end of a line had a fair chance to feel the crack of a whip directly on their skin. We were lined up in rows of five and we found ourselves at the end of the line. Because the group turned out to be more than 500, the surplus was cut off and sent back to camp "C", Klári and I included. Suddenly, we realized that we were back among the sick and ailing again.

We knew, of course, what that meant – what awaited us. The dreaded black trucks to cart the sick people away were expected shortly.

It was still daylight. Klári and I decided to escape from here.

Between the two blocks there was a latrine with thick excrement in it. We were counting the steps of the armed SS guard to time ourselves.

We had to wade through uncertain depths of the latrine while the guard turned his back on us. I don't quite remember how long we had to count before he turned back. Later in the evening we made an attempt and managed to get through without sinking into the faeces. It was only knee high. So we got through but we smelled something awful – the worst imaginable. Obviously, we didn't realize what we had to wade through.

In front of the barrack in camp "A" we found some sort of a puddle. One of us dipped into that. The other one found half a bucket of water and tried to scrape the thick, stinking mass off with that. Unfortunately, neither of us was very successful. We smelled so foul that the others refused let us come into the barrack. However, eventually, reluctantly, cursing and amidst abusing language, they let us stay. So we managed to end up in camp "A" again.

The train was about to leave with the labour transport the next morning. To our chagrin, because of our, still foul odour, nobody would accept us in a row of five. We were driven back from the gate again. We were back with the old and the sick again that is, those bound for the gas chamber.

I, too, almost gave up at that point. The black truck pulled up at three in the afternoon. An Austrian Wermacht soldier and the Gräser (commander of the camp) entered among the wailing, miserable people.

He said that another fifty people were needed for the transport of 500. Klári and I were luckily selected again from among the emaciated, the sick and old people. But at the gate, we were turned back again. Back in camp "C", we found an empty hospital barrack from where the patients had been taken to be gassed. In fact, the camp was almost totally empty. There were no guards around and spotting a shower-stall we entered. We took off all those stinking clothes, had a good shower at last and also washed our clothes clean. We put them on, all wet but not smelling any more and returned to the "hospital" barrack where we fell into a deep sleep, covered in blankets on the floor, warming one another. I don't know how long we slept but when I woke up I saw people marching outside. I kept on nagging Klári that we should join the crowd. By then, Klári had given up but I didn't let her. I grabbed hold of her hand and was tugging her along to come and fall in a line of five, together with three other people. We ran to catch up with the marchers.

It was at this point when fate decided to save us: at a small distance there were only three girls in a line who offered us a helping hand so we could join them.

One of them came from Marosvásárhely, her name was Sárika Mittler, and her friend Bella was also from Marosvásárhely. Klári recalls that the third girl's name was Judit. After so many attempts, we finally were in a row of five and managed to get through the gate and started out on a long, hard march from Birkenau to Auschwitz. We slept on the cold concrete at night. However, in the morning we were given clothes, clogs, underwear (!), caps (!) and a square tin number hanging on a string. My number was 839. We became the happy owners of warm socks, striped trousers and a jacket, underwear and a cap. We couldn't believe this earthly paradise. Our joy was completed by 250 grams of black bread together with some margarine.

I wished to wipe my mind clean of the memory of what happened to me in Birkenau. I never spoke about those horrors to anyone. An inner voice told me that nobody could understand these experiences except those who'd been through them. There's no use talking about it, even I wouldn't believe it was true...

Translation by Ágnes Merényi

Magda Sommer

Magda Summer, after the liberation returned to her town, Gyonk, Hungary. She matriculated from high school with excellent grades. In 1947-48 she enrolled in the medical faculty of the University of Pecs.

In 1949 she abandoned her studies and got married instead. She has two daughters – who are doctors, and four grandchildren.

Edit Kemény

THE „GOOD NAZI"

At about 8 o'clock in the morning a member of the Arrow-Cross turns up and selects ten women for work. I'm begging him with tears in my eyes to take me along too. I tell him I can cope even though I'm so small. He measures me with his eye, laughing, and then says okay. I'm glad because anything is better than waiting without a thing to do. We don't go very far, just to the opposite side of the square, to what used to be a Jewish house. Instead of Arrow-Cross men there are policemen at the entrance to the building and in the courtyard. They divide us up, we're supposed to tidy one of the apartments.

I stand at the front door frozen with horror. Cupboards ripped open, china broken, everything shattered, turned upside down. A thick layer of scattered documents, photos, papers and other bits and pieces are on the floor. I pick up trampled, crumpled letters and photographs one by one. Family photos: a little child smiles at me innocently, young people laughing, old-fashioned old people. There's chaos everywhere. Who knows how many destroyed family memories lie here? Nobody needs them any longer. Where are all these people? Where have they disappeared to? They suffer and struggle somewhere, torn apart from their families. Or maybe they're not even alive any more. But we must hurry. The policemen are watching us and some of them try to make small talk with us.

A few of the girls are encouraged by this and start nagging to be let off work. Some of them disappear and we think they've managed to get away, but then they drift back in, embarrassed, eyes cast down. One of the policemen comes up to me too, and after a few words he asks me to run him a bath upstairs and then wait for him there. He says he'll let me off afterwards. I'm thinking, should I go or not? What does he want with me? It would be wonderful to be free again, but at what price? Maybe he'd just send me back here like the others. And who can call him to account when he just laughs at me and refuses to keep his part of the bargain?

So I stay and keep on working. Everything looks bright and shiny by the evening. The best things are heaped together from various parts of the apartment, lovely pieces of furniture, paintings, Persian rugs and all the rest of it. We've made a really warm, soft nest for one of the chief gangsters to stay in to his heart's content and have the time of his life amongst all that beauty...

We're ready at last, this magnificent place is waiting for its lord to occupy it. We're also getting paid for our work: we're allowed to cook a little something for ourselves. There's some lard and flour and some potatoes in the pantry, our soup's ready within minutes. By the time we're lined up again we're no longer as hungry. The members of our little group are checked, eleven women, right, off we go! Two policemen escort us so that nobody escapes.

A young, blond smiling Arrow-Cross boy meets us half-way. "I'm coming to get them!" he calls out across the square and sends the other two away. We walk slowly, deep in thought. Suddenly he steps up close to me and says:

"You're not fourteen, dear, are you?"

"You're quite wrong", I answer, "I'm much older than that."

"It doesn't matter, please, say you're younger." He whispers so that the others can't hear. "Why?" I say, hating the idea of talking to him as I hate them all so much. But he insists: "Please, believe me, I mean no harm, don't be afraid of me, dear, I want to help you."

Meanwhile we arrive back at the house and as he leads us up the stairs he keeps saying, "Listen, make up your mind, before it's too late and come with me!"

Oh, my God! What should I do? I don't know. How can I possibly believe him? He's just another Arrow-Cross, just like all the others. God knows what he wants from me... But I haven't got time to think. The others disappear behind the door one by one while I stand there, silently, still hesitating. Then he takes my hand without a word and leads me upstairs, along corridors, I follow him as if unconscious, in a dream. Finally he stops in front of a door, presses my hand and smiles at me reassuringly. "Don't be afraid," he whispers and takes me in.

We cross a hall and arrive into a spacious room. I'm too astonished for words...here, in this bleak, gloomy house where hundreds are crying and wailing and trembling and moaning behind locked doors awaiting their sad fates, here is a place where everything's different. Here there's laughter and sweetness and playfulness and peace. There are twelve children of all ages, even a few toddlers with their mothers. Everyone stares at me. "I've brought you another girl, be nice and kind to her," he says.

They gather round me, offer me food, everybody's talking at once, asking my name and where I came from. They keep telling me that nobody will harm me here, the good Arrow-Cross man brings them food and toys. And before long the Red Cross will come and take us all away from here.

(...)

The next morning we're awakened by loud noises: slamming doors, crude swearing, yelling and screaming. All hell is breaking loose out there. We're huddled together silently, terrified, not daring to move. Seconds tick away in an agony of slowness, the maddening chaos slowly becomes more and more distant and soon a deadly silence enfolds the house. After a while we venture outside and look around in a shock. Windows and doors flung wide open, not a soul to be found, all those who were crying here only an hour ago have now disappeared.

(...)

The days drag on. It's more than a week since I've been here among the children. Nobody has asked me how old I am. I'm often afraid though when strange soldiers or Arrow-Cross men come by and look in on us, I'm afraid they'll spot me. But it looks as though I really don't seem any older, and besides I feel like a child, just like the others. And it's so good not to have to think, not to wonder, but to trust and hope, to believe in escape.

Meanwhile the house fills up and empties, again and again, over and over this grotesque comedy is played out. The Nazi thugs break in on us, thundering, yelling, waving their guns in the air, looking at us as if we were vermin, dizzy and drunk on their power. But when we say the magic words, "We're Red Cross children," they disappear at once. And then when the noise dies down we try to go on with whatever we were doing before.

As time passes almost every day more and more children and sometimes women arrive. It seems that our good Nazi, and one or two of his more decent brothers, snatches a child from each new transport. They bring them upstairs and quickly hand them over to us. Sometimes they manage to snatch a young mother with her baby from the group. We no longer have an abundance of food and space, three of us share a bed, but nevertheless we receive each newcomer kindly, we try to comfort them, dry their tears and share what we have.

(...)

December 6th, the *Day of Mikulás* arrives and the children can't wait for the evening because they've been promised a visit by Santa Claus. We clean, wash and iron all day. We tidy up the little ones, dress and comb them nicely. Most of us have just one set of clothes. I'm no exception either. But this refuge of ours is endlessly fruitful. The valuable stuff has of course long been taken away, but there are other things that are still of use to us. Old worn clothes, a nightgown, some linen, an old towel, a blanket, they all come in handy.

The little children are all clean and pretty, waiting breathlessly. The door opens and Santa Claus appears in a long red gown and a grey beard. The little ones greet him with loud cheers. We older ones recognize him at once, it's our good Nazi. They recite some nursery rhymes and sing songs for him. Then Santa gives them their little gifts: each child gets some sweets and biscuits. Who knows where he got them from... but this man has shown us that beneath the uniform there are also real human beings. He organized this little celebration just for the children, to bring some joy and happiness to their hearts, and smiles to their lips. We're all happy and carefree children again, and we're allowed to forget our crushing sadness, if only for a short while.

Translation by Ágnes Merényi

Edit Kemény

Edit Kemény is a mother of six children. She was a blue-collar worker all her working life. During the last few years she's been writing daily, documenting what happened to her during the war, and in the process she's even learnt to use a computer. This untold story is an excerpt from her book called "The Hard Years" which was published for her family. In 2006 she died at the age of 81.

Éva Rácz

WHEN I WAS TWELVE

My family lived a typically bourgeois Jewish life in Budapest before the war. My parents had a small underwear and children's clothing factory in Nefelejcs Utca, with 40 employees, and the firm also had an office with two rooms nearby in Garay Utca, and even a hansom cab. Later they had a car too to transport the clothes. We lived in Buda, in Karthauzi Utca, although my parents spent most of their time working in Pest in the 7th district. But my father had many friends, and he kept rather bohemian company, among them Rezső Seress and Jenő Rejtő.

At home it was my grandmother who ran the house and I grew up under her wings. I was given everything an only child of a middle-class family could have. I went to high school, had private lessons, and went to swim regularly, which later on proved to be extremely useful.

On March 19th, 1944 Germany occupied Hungary. My parents were just planning to celebrate their 17th wedding anniversary, which was on the 20th. The celebration did not take place, of course, and that was when I realized, at the age of 12, that there was serious trouble ahead!

At the factory, the sewing and embroidering machines had to be surrendered to the non-Jewish employees, and our apartment in the Karthauzi Utca was taken over by the Hungarian Gestapo which was headed by Péter Hain.

In May my father was drafted into forced labor service. The rest of the family had to move into a designated Jewish house marked out by a Star of David. Members of our family were already living in one such house, at 31 Népszínház Utca so we went there too. From then on, twelve of us lived in that four room apartment.

On October 15th, 1944 my father came home from forced labor camp weighing half as much as he did before he left. The Russians had liberated the camp in Szolnok so he escaped.

October 15th was also the day of the *proclamation. Several German tanks arrived in front of the house in Nepszinhaz Utca where we were living. The Germans said that someone from the building had fired on them, so they chased us all out into the street and herded us out to the race track. We were imprisoned there for two days. During this time the Hungarian Nazi regime consolidated power, and when they let us go we found that the house in Népszínház Utca was in ruins. And my father was made to return to forced labour camp.

We heard it was possible to get letters of protection from the Swiss government in Vadász Utca. After queuing, crowding and much anxiety we finally got our letter of protection! This piece of paper meant we could move into a „safe house" at Tátra Utca 47. Sixteen of us had to sleep in a small room, but we had hope!

In early November armed Hungarian Nazi thugs raided the house in Tátra Utca. They rang a bell in the courtyard. At that time there were only older people, some women and children left in the buiding. The men had all been taken away. The women under the age of 40 were then rounded up in the KISOK sports field and from there deported to camps in the West. My mother managed to escape just in time, just before reaching the border. (Later she managed to make her way back to the ghetto.) Then they drove the children out into the courtyard and then into the street. Many other children from other „safe houses" had also been rounded up there as well. We had to march to the bank of the Danube, which was not far from us. We were ordered to line up on the bank, and to take our coats and shoes off. Then they began to shoot us into the river, one by one.

They were almost out of ammunition. There weren't enough bullets to shoot all of us. So they tied three children together and shot the one in the middle so that the dead child would pull the other two into the water. What an invention!

I wasn't the one in the middle. I have no idea who was. I moved in the water almost unconsciously. I had slender wrists so I managed to disentangle my hands and then the rest of my body, and I began to swim. It was November, the water was horribly cold and dark. I stayed under the water as best I could, as they still had some bullets left to shoot at the moving heads they could see above water. I was racing against death, swimming for my life. I could only hear my tranier's words: „Never look back or to the side, only forward!"

After swimming for about two miles I climbed out of the water somewhere in Jozsefvaros, near Boráros Tér... But for a long time I was so exhausted that I could only pull one leg out of the water, no matter how icy it was.

It was early in the morning and the streets were dark and deserted. I found my way to the apartment of old friends of my father's in Gát Utca. I was barefoot and soaking wet. They took me in, dried me and thawed me out. It was a week before I was well enough to go out again.

But our friends in Gát Utca were already hiding several other Jewish people in their apartment, and they had a baby too. I didn't want to cause them trouble, so I left. I headed into the city to find somewhere else to hide.

I found myself in the Városliget, the city park, near the roundabout, where I bumped into one of our relatives. He was coming towards me with a bucket in his hand. It turned out that there was a concrete chamber underneath the roundabouts and he was hiding there.

I am not tall, and I was even smaller when I was 12... Perhaps I could also stay there for a while, we thought, but in the end it seemed more pactical for me to go on to the ghetto.

It wasn't such a bad idea after all because in the ghetto I found my mother. She was waiting in line for something, maybe bread?

I was not alone in the world any more. We somehow managed to last out, the two of us, until January 18th, 1945, when the Russians finally arrived and liberated the ghetto.

Translation by Bea Sándor

Éva Rácz
Éva Rácz lives in Budapest and works as a bookkeeper to this day. This story was dictated to her one time classmate Magda Kun.

Magda Kun

MEMORIES OF WONDER

This story begins with the face of a beautiful, young Transylvanian girl. A neat, well-proportioned figure, chiselled features, a pair of brown eyes radiating understanding and a flawless, candid smile. This is Lili, but her real name was Ilona Csákány.

I don't know where my uncle met her, but they fell in love, and their love overcame all obstacles, of which there were many. My grandfather's opposition in particular.

„A *shikse* in a Jewish family!" he'd grumble, „It's out of the question!"

We lived in Zugló, a suburb of Pest. My grandfather was the head of the family. My grandmother died of the Spanish flu towards the end of the First World War, so my grandfather had to raise their five children alone. His words had their weight, and with them he kept the family together. He met his grown up sons and son-in-laws every Sunday morning at the Turkish baths, and there they discussed family matters and world affairs.

The family ran a grocery store, and beside that a crop grinding business. Everyone worked hard, even from an early age. My mother was the youngest. When she was a child she had to climb up to the top of the carts that were loaded with huge sacks of meal and help the men lift the sacks onto their shoulders.

She was already a young wife when her brother told her about his secret relationship with Lili. My mother took pity on the lovers, and no one knows how, but with steady work she managed to soften up grandfather, until finally he gave in... And he was quite right too! Dear Lili turned out to be a blessing for the family, and my mother and Lili loved and helped one other till the end of their lives.

When the Anti-Jewish laws came into force the family business was transferred to Lili. Then from November 1st 1944 she hid our entire family in one room of their tiny apartment on Amerikai Utca. Eight of us lived there together. And then came a ninth, Lili and my uncle's new baby. She was born into turbulent times, under an unlucky star, on the night of October 15th. It seems that God must have been looking away when a stray piece of shrapnel flew in through the window of their apartment and hit the baby under her chin. Through shell-fire Lili ran to find a doctor, the baby almost bled to death, but they somehow managed to keep her alive. But half of her face remained permanently paralysed, and her sweet little smile was twisted into an unsightly grin. When she grew up she couldn't bear looking into mirrors. She died in an asylum forty years after the war.

A few weeks after the baby was born we were all still hiding in that tiny room when Lili got word that her younger brother had deserted the army and was being looked for by the military police. He'd been hiding in the crop grinding area and when they couldn't find him there they headed over to Lili's.

We hid as best as we could, squeezing ourselves together, hearts pounding with fear, certain they would search our room. Miraculously, they didn't! But it was a dangerous and narrow escape. After they left the entire family snuck out of the apartment and met outside in the KISOK sports field. It was winter, we stood there without our coats in the dreary cold, anyone could have seen us. We only dared go back when Lili came out for us. That was when my mother decided we could no longer stay there.

When we left the apartment, Lili gave my mother a great parting gift, a copy of her certificate of baptism.

Where were we to go now? It was getting dark. We headed into the city, hoping to find someone who would hide us. Eventually we found a friend who gave up her bed for us. I remember it was still warm when we lay down. The very next morning we had to leave as it wasn't safe to stay.

So we went in search of other friends near Csengery Utca, where we'd once lived. There was a family who'd rented one of the rooms in our apartment which they'd used as a tailor's workshop. They knew us well. They told us there was an office in the building of the Vigadó that arranged identification papers for Transylvanian refugees. They also supplied ration cards and resident permits! What luck that dear Lili was from Transylvania, and only a few years older than my mother!

Juci, the tailor's daughter, took us to the Vigadó and told the authorities we were her relatives from Transylvania, that we'd lost all our papers while escaping to Hungary and only managed to save one certificate of baptism. We were in luck, the story seemed credible. They gave my mother identification papers in the name of Ilona Csákány, an unmarried woman. I was added to her papers, her illegitimate child, Magda Csákány. To this day I've kept that invaluable piece of paper.

We had to memorize our new identities. From then on I was to be a fatherless bastard, and my mother was now born in Nagyborosnyó in 1906. (Her real name was Mrs. Béla Kramer, and she was born in Budapest in 1910.)

We went to Buda where no one knew us to look for a room. Through an acquaintance we found somewhere to live. The woman who rented us the room needed the money and she didn't ask too many questions, so our new address was 10 Attila Utca in the 1st district.

Our room was freezing cold and there was no way of heating it. When we weren't queuing for frozen potatoes or cabbages we had no choice but to lie in bed. There was a single bed with an iron frame in the room, and the only luxury our landlady could offer us was a rubber pipe which she filled with hot water from time to time. The saggy springs of that old mattress sent us rolling into the middle of the bed where we put the rubber pipe between us to warm our feet.

Around Christmas 1944 the Russians began bombing the outskirts of Buda. We were happy to hear them as we hoped they would bring us new life. But we had to hide our happiness in front of our landlady and her friends, who feared the barbarian Russians as we did the Germans. Some of them still believed in the arrival of „relief troops" promised by Hitler.

As the battles neared the city all the windows of the house were broken from the constant gunfire and the walls marked with bullet holes, so everyone moved into the cellars.

In the cellar we were given two benches and we put the mattress from our bed over them. There was an old laundry at one end of the cellar where the women cooked, if there was any water and anything to cook. There was a well two streets over and that's where my mother brought water from, often under gunfire. We washed ourselves in heated up snow, which always became filthy and black, but we had no choice. Someone, we didn't know who, broke into the ground floor shops and took some bottles of eau de cologne, which we used as disinfectant, and many rolls of toilet paper, which we draped over the pipes above our bed. It looked very cheerful.

There were German soldiers living in the building who told us that the tunnels under the castle just near us were packed with ammunition and that if they had to retreat they would blow everything up as they went! What a world! Only prayers could help.

The leaders in the cellar organized a daily prayer service, which one might say was ecumenical. We sang palms, we recited the Lord's prayer, we chanted the Litanies… I don't remember anything else, as these were the only ones I knew.

And how was it that I knew so many of these prayers? The answer lies in Vörösmarty Utca in the 6th district, at the Scottish Higher Elementary School which I'd attended for eight years. It was a very good school and I'm still grateful to them. They accepted many Jewish children and never tried to convert anyone. We even had Jewish studies classes twice a week. It was a mutually tolerant relationship.

What I learnt at that school saved our lives, as during all that time spent locked up together in the cellar, some people began to doubt our Transylvanian origins. But when I gave them a taste of my biblical knowledge and a performance of the Lord's prayer I think I convinced those Buda ladies there was no need to doubt our origins.

But we were constantly in danger, because my mother didn't know what I knew. So when prayers began I always made sure my mother sat opposite me so she could read my lips. The biggest danger, however, was that there were certain prayers during which I could hardly restrain myself. Lofty words describing Mary, such as „holy vessel", raised profane associations in that 12 year old girl I was then. Inside I was all giggles, and only the fear of death could control my laughter.

Fortunately, the Germans didn't have time to blow up the tunnels under the castle as they retreated. On February 13th 1945, my mother and I walked back to Pest.

What followed then belongs to another story.

Magda Kun

Magda Kun worked as a librarian and later as a journalist, with a special interest in children's literature. She remains active in retirement writing, editing, organizing and consulting on cultural events.

Zsuzsa Gábor

ROMEO 1944

My grandfather's real name was Izidor Lichter, but to me he will always be remembered as my guardian angel. In death, however, he also became known as Romeo. My guardian angel was a wise, energetic, well-informed old man. He'd fought in the First World War and had been through a lot. He was a retired printer and a trade unionist. He was bald and chubby, with a scarred face and a hot temper. When someone needed to be taught a lesson his thundering voice would fill the apartment building where we lived and where he was the caretaker. But he was responsible and firm in his actions. His care and understanding could always be counted on. And above all he loved his meek, softly spoken, gentle-eyed old wife dearly.

This story begins at the end. Romeo died at the age of 73, on October 15th 1944, in Budapest, a father of five children, and grandfather of many, on the day of Horthy's proclamation. The day began with unexpected joy. In the morning, on hearing Horthy's proclamation everyone thought that the war was over, at least in Hungary. On the ground floor of the big, grey block with the circular galleries where we lived, someone put a radio in an open window so that we could all hear the latest news. An overjoyed Jew went out into the street and told the first Arrow-Cross man he met to run because they were starting to round them up down the road.

In the evening the news of Szálasi's coup drove us to despair. Only women, children and a few elderly men lived in the house. The men gathered in the courtyard to discuss whether they should mount some kind of a guard at the building entrance and use clubs for weapons, but nothing came of it.

That night two gunshots rang out in the dark, one in the street and one in the courtyard. Within seconds German and Hungarian Nazis burst into the building, banging furiously on the tin letter boxes by the entrance to announce their presence. They yelled at us in German, "Everyone downstairs now! Hands up! Double quick!" We were so scared we didn't even grab our bags with our bare necessities which were packed and ready in the hall.

More gunshots could be heard from some of the flats, and as it turned out later, only the lucky ones made it out. Wherever the Nazis met even minimal resistance, they just gunned people down.

18 dead bodies were left in the house.

The rest – mothers with toddlers and helpless old people among them – were herded down Aradi Utca, then Teréz Korut, as far as the school in Nagyatádi-Szabó Utca (re-named Kertész Utca after the war) with their arms in the air. At that time the building had a door leading to the cellar from the street (it has since been walled up). On either side of the staircase leading to the cellar German soldiers were lined up and gave each of us entering a sickening kick. Then we were shoved into a large, white-washed cellar and beaten and thrashed regardless of age or anything. They used helmets, truncheons and pieces of wood and did not stop till blood was shed. They told us they were looking for arms.

A piece of biscuit wrapped in paper was found in my 18 year old cousin's pocket. They wanted to cram it into his mouth, together with the paper, but he resisted and was beaten to death in front of his own mother.

When they'd let off some steam they poured bleach on the bloodied floor, picked the men out of the mess, and crammed them into another part of the cellar. Their screams and cries could be heard all night long. No one ever saw them again, dead or alive.

The rest of us were lined up facing the wall. We had to stand with our arms held up for hours on end. Meanwhile the German soldiers guarding us kept cocking their guns, just to remind us that we could be shot at any moment. Death was everywhere.

A 14 year old boy with a girlish face had somehow been left among the women. When the soldiers caught sight of him he was dragged away to an empty part of the cellar. They drew a circle at eye level with a dot in the middle and ordered him to stare at it. Whenever the soldiers wanted to have a little fun they yelled at him so that he turned around and then they and kicked his skinny legs with all their might.

They found other amusements as well. A young orthodox boy with a kippah and tzitzes sticking out from under his shirt was shoved in from the street. They made him confess that he was hiding arms under his shirt, in his his tzitzes. While grilling him they kept banging his head with a chair. It made a horrifying sound. Then he was taken away.

It was dark again when the women were all herded out into the street. Long streams of people were hanging around out there but we couldn't see who was who in the dark.

A Tiger tank followed the last row of women. Every so often it switched its lights on and accelerated. Certain that they were going to get crushed the women rushed forward in a panic, tripping and falling into the other women.

"They're taking us to the Danube!" the women said. Fear spread from mouth to mouth like wildfire. But eventually we ended up in the synagogue on Rumbach Sebestyén Utca. We filled up the entire building, the ground floor, the gallery, everywhere. There may have been one or two toilets and a couple of taps for all those people. Within a very short space of time the situation became unbearable. There was no food, no one said a word, no one knew anything. There were corpses behind the ark. And the synagogue's roof which was made of glass was a constant source of terror to us, if there was an air-raid, we thought, that would be the end of us all! A permanent fear of death hung over us.

It lasted for two days, then we were released.

Meanwhile at our apartment building, Romeo's daughter had somehow managed to escape shortly after we'd been rounded up and then made it back to her father. Romeo came out of the cellar and asked his daughter, "Where's Mama?" "Mama's been taken away," she answered, and before she could say anything more the old man collapsed and died. He was the 19th victim of that day.

Later, my grandmother came back, like Juliet, to find her husband dead...

Translated by Ágnes Merényi

Zsuzsa Gábor

Zsuzsa Gábor has worked all her life in business, first as an employee and later she ran her own company. She has two grown up sons and three grandchildren. She lives in Budapest. This story was dictated to Magda Kun.

Olga Sólyom

RUSSIAN CABBAGE SOUP

Although I'm over 70 years old now, it's still difficult for me to talk about what happened when I was a 10 year old child. It's difficult emotionally and also because it's so deeply personal. The tragedy I lived through is my very own and it's painful to think that it might be compared to anyone else's because the experience was unique. Although this is not easy to explain, the time has come to tell our stories, for our children and grandchildren, so that they will know and remember and continue to bear witness. So, how should we tell our stories so that others will understand, so that they will be real and not seem like just another newspaper article or chapter in a history book? And even if we succeed in doing this, can we ever make others feel what we felt in this time?

I adored my father, for whom I was everything, his only child. I can still feel his hand holding mine as he took me to school when I was 6. It wasn't far away from home, but we always started earlier so that we could walk for a little longer, just the two of us. He would talk and joke and we laughed a lot. For me this was happiness itself.

It didn't last long. I was 7 years old when he was first taken away for forced labor service. On Sundays my mother and I would go and visit him in Nagytarcsa where the camp was so that we could spend a few hours with him. Those other Sundays, those days when we visited my father's family in the mornings, just the two of us, seemed to be gone forever.

Then came 1944 and with it the Nazi occupation of Hungary. I cried as I looked out of our third floor window, I watched him until I lost sight of him. He was walking slowly, he was wearing a parka and he was carrying some kind of a backpack. I understood, I knew, even then, that I might not see him again.

And so it went on. We were made to move into a house marked with a Star of David. These were houses that the Nazi authorities had branded with a Magen David and into which Jews, who were driven out of their own homes, were forced to live. We were only allowed to leave these houses for a few hours a day. This was the predecessor of the ghetto.

We moved into 40 Ó street, into an apartment with three rooms that belonged to a distant relative of ours. 20 or 25 of us were packed into that flat. We felt trapped, forced to be together, in constant fear. It was a terrible feeling, and even though we were only children, these things quickly made adults of us.

Then October 15th arrived. It was a Sunday, and the forced labor servicemen who were in Budapest were given a few hours off. We were listening to the radio with my father at noon. We heard Horthy's proclamation and we rejoiced, thinking that the war was over. But just a few hours later we were overcome by despair. We begged my father to stay with us, not to go back to the camp, but he said he had to go as they'd been told that if anyone deserted then the rest of the company would be decimated. I never saw him again.

So we stayed there in the house with the star. We knew that every day Hungarian Nazis raided these houses and took the people away somewhere. Whenever a car stopped in front of the house we got ready to leave, which meant putting on as many layers of clothing as we could, because we knew they would take everything away from us.

With a Swiss pass we eventually managed to get into the so-called internationally protected compound in Kolumbusz Utca. We were put up in temporary shanties, many of us on the floor, sitting on wooden benches, lying like herrings. We had to wash ourselves outside in freezing cold water in temperatures well below zero. All of us were vaccinated against typhus which made me ill. I got a soaring fever and we had no medication at all, but I survived. The international protection of course did not prevent the Hungarian Nazis from raiding there too. They rounded up crowds of mostly women, children and older people, and they selected the women who were fit for work and then took them away, we didn't know where. My mother was among them. I stayed there with my aunt, who had managed to stay behind, and my little cousin. Later we were herded into the ghetto.

13 Klauzál Square was our next address. We lived on the third floor of what was once a beautiful old house. Every day I tried to kill myself by

jumping out the window. I didn't want to live without my father and my mother. My poor aunt was in utter dispair since she was responsible for me now. I don't know how but she managed to find out that our cousin was working for the International Red Cross. She went to see her and begged her to somehow find my mother because she didn't know what to do with me. Three days later my mother arrived.

Fortunately she was still being held in Budapest and my cousin helped her to escape.

After this, my mother and aunt decided that we couldn't stay and wait until the ghetto was liquidated. They thought if we didn't escape we would be killed there. Some Christian families were still moving out of the houses that were to become part of the ghetto, so seizing the opportunity we jumped behind one of the carts loaded with their things and pretended to be helping them push it, and so we walked out of the ghetto through Csányi Utca.

For the next five weeks we hid like hunted animals. The suffering was almost indescribable.

The first place we went to was the Star of David house on Ó' Utca where we'd once lived. The janitor of the building was an exceptional man who tried to help us as much as he could. He gave us refuge as often as possible and would warn us if there was trouble. And even though he couldn't hide us, in the end he found us somewhere we could hide. We could only stay there for one night as he'd warned us that some Nazis had moved into apartments in the building.

Our next hiding place was the basement of an abandoned furniture factory on Kisfaludy Utca. The basement was divided into two levels. We were squeezed into the upper level which proved crucial. The only reason we could stay there was because some corrupt Hungarian Nazis were extorting money from us in exchange for „protection". Once in the middle of the night they stormed in and ordered us under threat of death (being shot into the Danube to be precise) to raise 10,000 pengos. Somehow we managed to get them what they demanded. Then one day, when Pest had already been under attack for some time, a bomb hit the cellar. Everything shook around me, plaster and bricks went flying, whole walls collapsed, and terrifying minutes went by when I called out for my mother and no answer came. Miraculously we were spared, but the people underneath us all died or were wounded. Only the four of us got away unharmed.

We went to hide in another part of the building, but it was also hit by a bomb, so the next day we had to escape again. The situation was extremely dangerous, as anyone who was out in the streets after dark was shot. One night we hid in a public toilet. Every moment we were afraid someone would come in and find us.

Then my aunt had the idea that we should claim an abandoned Jewish apartment. It took unbelievable daring. The two women went to the local authorities and told them that they'd just escaped from the advancing Russian army and were with two children and needed somewhere to stay. They pulled my cousin's cap down to his nose so that they wouldn't notice his red hair and his freckles. And, wonder of wonders, they gave us an apartment in Aradi Utca. We were in a terrible state when we got there. It was unbearable to think that we were going into a Jewish flat, not knowing what had happened to its owners. On the other hand the thought of having nowhere to go again that night was terrifying. We children felt these things too, but for our mothers it was surely even worse.

We made it into the apartment, but we were terribly hungry and there was no heating. We didn't dare turn on the lights for fear of being noticed and we were so afraid of the bombings.

My aunt dared to go out into the street and she brought back some potatoes which she'd stolen from somewhere. Just as we began to cook them, a Hungarian Nazi who was in charge of the house came and told us that unless we presented our identification papers within an hour proving that we were not Jews, he would have us taken away. We dropped everything and disappeared. Decades after that night, my cousin and I still say that this is one of our most horrible wartime memories: that we had to leave the food behind that we'd been so desperate for.

We had to hide again, in public toilets, anywhere, to spend the nights somewhere. On one of the last days of the battle for Budapest my mother thought of someone who lived on Róbert Károly Utca who might hide us. We left the house on O Utca and ran along Lehel Utca from Ferdinánd Bridge. There were only houses on one side of the street so we were especially vulnerable to bombs, shells and machine gun fire. We stayed close to the houses, huddled together, moving as fast as we could, praying to die together if we were hit. This is how we got to Aréna Utca (which is Dózsa György Utca today), which we discovered was the actual frontline of the battle for the city and so impossible to cross. We couldn't stay there as we surely would have been shot. We had no choice, we had to go back where we came from, along the exact same route.

To walk this distance (from Ó Utca to Dózsa György Utca) takes almost an hour, for an adult. I can scarcely imagine how long it took us then, how we managed, the shape we were in, exhausted both physically and mentally, going back to a completely hopeless situation.

It was the janitor in Ó Utca who saved us again. Before the war the area had been full of prostitutes. The janitor knew one of them who had just given birth and needed the money, so she took us into her apartment in Rózsa Utca. She would dip the baby's pacifier in poppy tea so he wouldn't cry all the time. Mostly it was my job to cradle him.

These were the last days of the war and we had nothing to eat at all. When the first Russian soldier came into the cellar on Rózsa Utca and ascertained that „nyemci nyet", there are no Germans, he looked at me lying on some rags, looking quite dead. He asked what was the matter with me and my mother told him that I hadn't eaten for four days and was too weak to get up. He went out and came back with a mess tin full of *shchi*, Russian cabbage soup. My mother measured it out with a teaspoon and we ate it for days. It was wonderful, I can't ever forget that taste. Since then I've eaten in many Russian restaurants, always looking for that same taste, but never finding it again.

I asked my son once, when he was 16, whether he could imagine what it meant to be really hungry. He said that if he was hungry he'd take something to eat out of the fridge. And if there's no fridge, I asked? Then he'd go to the local store and buy something. And what if there are no stores, nothing in them, no streets, nowhere to go? He told me that he couldn't imagine that at all. I understood then that the things we lived through are incomprehensible, even to me, and to today I do not know how we managed to survive.

Translation by Bea Sándor

Olga Sólyom

Olga Sólyom was born in Budapest in 1934 into a Reform Jewish family. She went to a Jewish elementary and high school. In 1957 she received her university degree in Economics as well as languages. In 1977 she also received a degree in International Business and that same year she earned her PhD. She's been retired since 1989. She was a founding member of the Alliance of Hungarian and Israeli Friends and for several years she also worked for "Blue Line", a telephone hot-line for children and teenagers.

Judit Patak

LIFE IS BEAUTIFUL, ISN'T IT?

Langenbielau, Friday April 27th , 1945

It's my 18th birthday. I wake with uncertain senses. Outside the sunshine is sparkling, soft and warm. Inside I am rotting in these loathsome barracks. I'm awfully hungry, as usual. I can hardly wait till lunch. This week we're on the afternoon shift. This means we get our plate of *turnip soup at half past eleven and start at the factory at one.

Nowadays we rarely hear the sounds of gunfire. But the hope we'd felt has receded and life has gone back to our daily routine. According to some rumors the battles are continuing, far away. It's also said that the Soviets are already close to Berlin. So why is nothing happening in Langenbielau…?

I'm hanging around in the courtyard where a few blades of lean, rank grass grow. I guess you could call it grass, or flowers, but really they're barely weeds. I'm enjoying my new shoes. I got them on Tuesday, on my father's birthday, from the Romanian factory master. Surely it was Daddy who sent them, it was his way of sending a sign of life, that he was still alive and urging me not to lose heart. It won't last for long.

But it was very lovely, the way the factory master gave me the shoes. It's around ten o'clock in the evening when he comes over to the side of the machine where I'm working. From there the guard sitting at the end of the room can see him perfectly well. Waving his arms about furiously he shouts at me: "Abstellen!" By now I already know this means the machine has to be switched off. I do it, even though it's not broken. He tinkers with it a bit, and then orders me not to touch it, saying that one of the discs don't work. He leaves with a stern face. The machine stays idle till the end of the shift. It's understandable that the machines require extraordinary care, for on one of them gas masks are made, on the other silk parachutes are woven. With materials of this kind there must not be even the slightest weaving fault. When the guard, the barking Berliner, bawls at me because the machine is stopped, I say what I'm told: "There's a broken disc." And at the same time I'm so scared, what happens if he re-starts it?

On the following Tuesday evening the same thing happens again with the machine, only this time the factory master comes over with a bunch of tools under his arm and throws something down on the platform between the two machines. This "something" lands heavily. Then he crouches down and suddenly there appear a pair of shoes. Real brown Oxfords, almost new, and they even have laces. He shouts at me to get down and help him, and as I do he whispers: "Put them on at once." I bend over and step into them. My hands are trembling so much I can hardly tie the laces. By the time I stand up my old wooden clogs are nowhere to be found. They've disappeared, together with the tools.

I stand stiffly between the two machines. One of them clacks and clatters, the other one stands silently as ordered. There is a strange, inexplicable pleasure in my heart. I want to run around the factory and shout out to the girls: "Look here. I've got real shoes!" But of course it's prohibited to leave the machine and besides, God forbid anybody should know about them! So I stand there, and slowly the tears begin to fall.

On the way back to the barracks I discover that the shoes are a bit loose as my heels come out. I bend down for a moment and tighten the laces.

Just then the dinner bell wakes me from my daydreaming. I'm about to keep heading to the barracks when Klári comes by and hands me my soup-plate. (Actually this "soup-plate" is an earthenware bowl that can hold just over half a litre of watery soup). "Thanks," I say and join the queue with her. Then we walk back with the full bowl in our hands. At the door to the barracks I am stopped still, rooted to the spot.

In this room twenty of us live together. To one side of the room, beside our pallets which lie on the ground, there's a window under which stands a long trestle table made of rough board with kitchen stools around it. Normally there's nothing on the table. But now it's laid with some kind of whitish sheet. Everybody is sitting on her stool and looking at me. I walk over to my place and see another full bowl there. But my soup-plate is still in my hands. How has the other one got there? All around the bowl are laid fifteen if not twenty sandwiches. Little slices of bread with margarine, artificial honey, a piece of ripe cheese, a slice of unpeeled potato fished out of the soup and boiled turnip.

Éva stands up and clears her throat and as she wishes me happy birthday her eyes mist over with tears. Then she recites a little verse from one of her poems as she often does.

"Well, let the birthday party begin," says Tildi. We sit down and eat. Meanwhile, I ply them with questions: how did they get so much food? And they confess: the sandwiches are collected from their own little, narrow portions. But that bowl of soup! A whole bowl! The dish was borrowed and everybody poured a few spoons of their own soup into it until the bowl was full. My God, I burst into tears even today when I think of it!

Of course, I instantly begin to cry. "Don't cry," says Zsuzsa, "look here instead, now comes the real surprise!" And then she pulls out the most wonderful pinafóre! It's grey and has a gathered skirt, and on the left side of the bodice are my initials "PJ" embroidered in red and blue. All stitched by hand and buttons too! Who knows where they got all this stuff from!

"Try it on!" they urge. I do. It's a perfect fit! "How did you make it?" Then Zsuzsa, who'd been a dressmaker before the war tells me that she'd secretly taken my measurements. Then I remember how earlier she'd been playing with a piece of string and telling me what a wasp waist I was and giving me all kinds of advice on what style of dress I should wear to my next ball.

So here, in the deep darkness of the barracks, in the grey desert of my soul, the flowers of pleasure and smiles flourish. A fairy's hopeful fingers had stroked our dull hair and pale faces. We were young... I still have that dress with me today.

Translation by Iván Vadász

Judit Patak

On June 11, 1944, at the age of 17 she was deported to Auschwitz. From August 1944 until May 9, 1945 she was in a forced labor camp in Langenbielau working at a textile factory owned by Christian Dierig. She was the only member of her family to have survived the deportations. Upon her return she matriculated from high school and in 1950 she earned her Diploma of Education. She became a high school teacher in mathematics and physics. She was a teacher all her entire working life. Now she is retired and a grandmother of five.

Judy Weiszenberg Cohen

A MOST MEMORABLE KOL NIDRE

Fragments of Memories

Practicing Judaism or celebrating any Jewish Holiday was totally forbidden by the Nazis at the Auschwitz-Birkenau death camp. The Nazis knew it would give solace to the prisoners. So we weren't allowed to mark any Jewish occasion.

But this particular year, in 1944, when I was there, one day, some of the older women – and by older I mean they could have been 35 or 40 years old (to a 15 year old anyone who is over 30, looks old) – asked these two specific Kapos (high-ranking prisoners) for permission to do something for Kol Nidre (the Eve of Yom Kippur.)

Most of the Kapos (prisoners with authority)were really brutalized and brutal people but a few of them remained truly kind. We knew these particular two were approachable. One of the kind Kapos, I remember, was a tall, blonde Polish woman, non-Jewish. The other one was a little red-headed, young woman, a Jewish girl from Slovakia.

The women told them that we wanted to do something for Kol Nidre. The little red-headed girl, Cirka (or Cila) I believe was her name, but I am not sure, was simply amazed that anyone still wanted to pray in that hell-hole called, Birkenau. "You crazy Hungarian Jews" she exclaimed. "You still believe in this? You still want to do this and here?"

Well, we did.

So, we asked for and received, one candle and one siddur (prayer book). We were about 700 women jam-packed in one barrack. Everybody came: the believers, the atheists, the Orthodox women, the agnostics, women of all descriptions and of every background. We were all there.

The two Kapos gave us only ten minutes and they were guarding the two entrances to the barrack to watch out for any SS guard who might happen to come around – unexpectedly.

Then, someone lit this lone candle – and a hush fell over the barrack. I can still see this scene: the woman, sitting with the lit candle, started to read the Kold Nidre passage in the siddur. Incredibly, all of this happened in a place where, we felt, it was appropriate that instead of we asking forgiveness from God, God should be asking for forgiveness from us.

And yet, we all wanted to gather around the woman with the lit candle and siddur.

She recited the Kol Nidre very slowly, so that we could repeat the words if we so desired.

But we didn't. Instead, the women burst out in a cry – in unison. Our prayer was the sound of this incredible cry of hundreds of women. It seemed to give us solace. Remembering Yom Kippur was somehow a reminder of our homes, and families because this was one Holy Day that was observed even in the most assimilated homes.

Something happened to these women. It was almost as if our hearts burst. I never heard either before or since then such a heart rendering sound.

Even though no one really believed the prayer would change our situation, that God would suddenly intervene – we weren't that naïve – but the opportunity to cry and remember together helped us feel better. It reminded us of our former, normal lives; alleviated our utter misery, even for a littlest while, in some inexplicable way.

Even today, many decades later, every time I go to Kol Nidre services, I can't shake it.

That is the Kol Nidre I always remember.

Judy Weiszenberg Cohen

Judy Weiszenberg Cohen was born in Debrecen, Hungary, in 1928 as the youngest of seven siblings.

In 1944, she was deported with most of her family members to the Nazi death camp of Auschwitz-Birkenau. She survived this and subsequent camps, such as Bergen-Belsen and the slave labour camp of Achersleben.

She immigrated to Canada in 1948 and initially worked in the garment industry. After additional schooling at a business school she changed to doing office work.

While raising a family, she pursued her non-credit education at various universities and colleges. She has become active in the field of Holocaust and anti-racism education with public speaking. She has created the web site "Women and the Holocaust".

Anna Lázár

DOUBLE STORY

In 1938, at the time of the Anschluss my father felt that we had to leave Hungary. He was wanted by the military police, so we emigrated to France. My father's youngest brother, Béla Lazarovits, had been living there for some time in Grenoble. In the beginning we stayed at their place.

All my life my father raised me to become what he was, a leftist. A short while after our arrival I joined the illegal leftist anti-fascist youth movement. In 1943, when I was fourteen, our group began to undertake a more active resistance against the German occupiers, even armed guerrilla fighting. I became a mediator among the Austrian, Italian, Hungarian, Jewish and Spanish groups. A number of armed groups were formed. These needed to be connected and information exchanged among them so that those in charge should meet as seldom as possible, as these meetings were a threat to the movement. Armed members operated underground in isolation and only came together for specific actions. The French locals supported the resistance. A lot of people in the villages gave food to the partisans or provided hiding places for them. Certain policemen even let it be known that they'd be carrying food ration coupons on a certain route to a certain village and stopping at certain places along the way... Armed groups drew up schedules of where to detonate explosives and we had to be informed about this in time. My job was to meet the heads of the groups in question and to relay them details daily. I jotted down the time and place of explosions on cigarette papers and as I was good at mathematics I embedded them into long algebraic formulas. I would roll up the paper tight and stick it into the handlebar of my bike under the rubber cap. After I'd made contact I would swallow the paper. Cigarette papers were easy to roll up and easy to swallow...

Once I was entrusted with an extremely dangerous task: hand grenades had to be carried over the demarcation line. Who was to carry them? Obviously, the girl of fifteen. But I wasn't even a member of the party yet! My superiors had decided that I, as a fifteen year old, was no longer a child and so ready for the job. I carried the grenades strapped to the back of my bike. When I got to the German border I was told to get off the bike and the German soldier asked me, "What are you carrying there on that bicycle, dear?" To which I answered with a poker face, "A bomb." The German started laughing, slapped my bottom and waved me through...

But I must confess, that was all just a fairy tale!
My friend and companion in France, Gizi Révai, began spreading this story about me in Budapest after the war when we returned. At the time I was still only seventeen and a half and one could only apply for Party membership from the age of eighteen. So Gizi invented the story about the explosives so I would be given special permission to join early. She told everyone about those explosives I'd carried over the border on my bike... even Nok Lapja, the women's magazine, wrote a story about me.

I did carry a number of things to a number of places, but no explosives, as far as I know.

Hungarian leftist expatriates in Geneva regularly sent money to Hungarians in France, so I often had to go to the French-Swiss border in the Alps on my bike. True, there was a packing case on the back of my bike, but it was mostly filled with food and, of course, money. Not that I was going on a picnic... It's true that I went to Lyon by bike as my friend Gizi used to tell it. But in fact I never carried very important secret materials. Because you see my superiors had changed their minds and withdrawn that task from me. They probably thought it too dangerous for me, even if I was no longer a child, trains were being blown up all over the place. So they changed my commission: I was to teach my boss, Ervin Gazdag (father of Gyula Gazdag the film director) to ride a bike... I did teach him, but it was torture and agony. He was a very slow learner! In the end he somehow managed and went to Lyon with a packing case strapped to the back of his bike. When he came back his face was bright flaming red. The sun had been beating down all the way and he was burnt to a crisp. He blamed me for his exhaustion and sunburn, saying that I hadn't warned him it was so hard to ride a bike so far in such heat...

So that's the real story behind the lie. However, there's ***another*** *true version of this story.*

We lived in an occupied town in France and the Germans randomly closed down streets with wire fences. Those who were caught in between these "borders" were stopped and had their identity papers checked. Once I got caught. My bike had two cases strapped onto the back for deliveries, and my schoolbooks and other things would be piled on top of the cases. The soldiers at the check-point asked me, "What are you carrying there, sweetie?" To which I replied, "Bombs." The soldiers were young Polish boys with downy chins – Polish paramilitary youth were often recruited from the occupied territories for these kinds of jobs – and we were about the same age. "Right, then go ahead!" they said laughing and let me through...

Translated by Ágnes Merényi

Anna Lázár
At the end of the war, aged 17, Anna returned from France with her parents. She finished high school, then went on to university where she became a historian. She also worked as an interpretor in several languages, as well as a translator. In 1982 she published her book "Hungarians in the Worker's Movement in France". She lived in Budapest with her husband, her two daughters and her two granddaughters. She died in 2004.

Vera Szöllős

WE SURVIVED
(Excerpts)

1.

Silently but firmly the door shuts in our face. We're left there stranded in the corridor. Dad and mum look at each other over my head. "Let's go," Dad said, 'there's nothing for us here."

We slump silently along the familiar corridor. All the doors and windows are shut. Nobody comes out. I think I feel the neighbors watching our shame from behind their tightly drawn curtains.

The corridor seems endlessly long. It feels as if ages have past since we rang the bell of our flat, the one we were forced to leave a year before. A stranger opens the door.

"Good afternoon," my father says, "we've just come home from the deportation. We used to live here before that." The expression on the woman's face grows hard. "It's our home now" she answers and slams the door.

The neighbours withdrew behind their curtains a year ago too, when we were forced into the ghetto.

We turn the corner and walk past the Kerepes' flat.

Laci Kerepes was my best friend in the house. We did everything together. His mother was a strict woman. She used to beat up Laci regularly and made him kneel on dry corn for every petty little thing. I wondered if he was peeping from behind the curtain too.

We get out into the street at last. My parents aren't talking. We go back to our temporary shelter: the tiny sixth floor room of the Korona Hotel. Gasping from the long flights of stairs we've just climbed, we sit down on our makeshift beds.

"We have to leave here," says Dad finally, "I'll find a room and then we'll see if we can find a flat of our own."

At noon we go to the cafe. It's maintained by the *Joint.* The Joint give us clothes as well, even the ones we're wearing, because our own were worn out and ragged by the time we got home. The Joint is operated by *The American Jewish Joint Committee.*

In the canteen Dad talks to a man who knows of a room. He suggests we take a look. We go there straight after lunch. We're in luck. The room is still available. It's furnished too, which is important, because we don't have our own furniture. We'll have to go to the big synagogue. That's where all the furniture and other things belonging to the Jewish community were dumped, the leftover items that weren't hauled away by others.

We move in the same day. The flat belongs to an old lady who lives alone. She allows us to use the bathroom for cooking. We have to cross it anyway to get to our room. We heat up the bathroom and soak ourselves in the bath for at least half an hour each.

The next morning we go to the synagogue. All sorts of furniture and carpets are piled up there in a mess. Quite a lot of people are looking around but we don't see anyone familiar to us.

But we find granny's old armchair and her big Persian rug as well. It's a dingy old carpet with hardly any pile left on it. My parents roll it out to make sure it's hers. Someone has cut half a meter off at one end. Mum crouches down to roll the rug back up. "Must have been the Russians", she says, "They must have cut it off." Why the Russians? What on earth would the Russians want with the end of granny's rug? Granny hasn't come back yet. We haven't heard anything. Mum has been asking everybody who was taken with the first transport. We went with the third. Went? Were taken.

We were driven out into the trucks. Then out of the trucks and into the camp. Then, into the fertilizing unit and out of the fertilizing unit in our own, hardened clothes. Then, onto the train and out to a brick factory to work. My parents carried raw bricks to the drying unit. A brick like that weighed at least twenty kilos. We children studied with a teacher in a warm room on the top of the factory's furnace. I already knew the teacher from my previous school. She wasn't our teacher though, she was teaching grade three.

We, in grade one, were taught by a beautiful, twenty-year-old girl. She used to bring in colourful beads, sticks and disks in a huge box and used them to help us learn arithmetic. We had a reading book, too. All white and azure green. Pictures and letters. In one of the pictures a Jewish family was observing Sabbath. The mother, with a shawl over her head, was lighting a candle. The father was standing there, wearing a little hat, and two children in nice, smart clothes were watching the candles. It was interesting. I had no idea at all where people like this lived. We never used to do anything like this at home.

At home. I wonder who lives in our home now? I wonder where my bed is? I wonder where the biscuit tin is in which I had put all my important things in case there was an air-raid alarm at night and I would just have to grab it and take it down with me. Adults take their important things with them too. I had my pressed flowers in the tin, which we'd picked with Dad on our excursions, my colour pencils, a notebook and a little marzipan.

Now we lived here, amongst unfamiliar furniture. Mum is making pancakes and doughnuts. The bathroom is filled with the smell of cooking lard and it is seeping into the room as well. Dad will start work at the bank in a couple of days, the same bank he'd been fired from because of the anti-Jewish Laws. Mum says we'll have to start studying soon so that I won't loose a year at school. If I take my second year exams at the end of the summer, I can start grade three in September.

I don't understand why it's so urgent. If it has to be year two, let it be year two. Mum says that we could go to the outdoor swimming pool and study there. Everybody's having a summer vacation, only I have to be studying. Obviously, those who were not deported don't have to study in the summer by the outdoor swimming pool. I wonder what the others were doing while we were away? We? All the Jewish people. Everybody from our transport came back. Hardly anyone has come back from the other two transports yet. I don't know where they could be.

It took us almost two weeks to get home from Czechoslovakia by train and we've been home for about two weeks now. You can make it home even from America in that time, even though there's the ocean to cross between us.

I get two presents from Dad. One is a small flat box with little dice in it. Each of them has a number painted on them. The box is not full, there is place for one more little dice in there. Using this space you have to shift the dice so that they form a nice row. One, two, three, and so on. It's a good game but it's not easy.

The other game is a box of sticks. You have to hold the sticks in your fist tight, stand them on the table and then let them fall. They fall all over the place in a mess, one straw on top of the other. Then you have to pick them up one by one, making sure that none of the other sticks move. It's difficult to do, but my parents always help. I always play with my parents. I haven't seen any children here in the house yet. We hardly ever meet other people. But then, I don't want to go anywhere anyway.

I had a bad experience before the deportation. One day Laci and I went to play at Pista Balogh's place. He had his own room, and it was good to play there, we didn't disturb anyone. His mother let me in but somehow she was different than she usually was. We'd barely begun to play when Mum turned up. She was breathless. She apologized and took me home immediately. Pista's mother didn't object. Mum told me on the way home why I had to leave. We're not allowed to go out on the street without the yellow star, she said, every Jew has to sew a big yellow star onto their clothes. I wasn't wearing one on mine. If you don't wear the star and a Christian realizes that you're a Jew there could be big trouble.

In the afternoons we go out for walks with Mum. Sometimes we have a pastry at the bakery. I don't know anybody at the playground. I wonder what's happened to my friends?

2.

I had a nightmare. I was sitting under grandma's piano and then it turned out that it was a gas chamber. I was sniffing in the air but couldn't smell anything. I wanted to climb out but I couldn't. I woke up. Mum and Dad were asleep at the other end of the room. But are they really there? Maybe I'm alone? I get up and tiptoe over to their bed. I touched Dad's face. It's warm. Slightly startled, he opens his eyes.

"What is it?" he asks.

"Nothing."

Dad sits up and strokes my hair.

"Everything is all right son. Go back to bed and try to sleep."

I felt more awake now than before. I climb back into my bed.

Of course they thought I'd been asleep, earlier in the evening when Auntie Olga came to visit. She used to go to school with Mum. She also just got back from deportation, but not from the same place as us.

My parents and Auntie Olga were talking quietly under the dim light of the table lamp. Mum was crying. She was blowing her nose and with a choke in her voice she said: "I cannot believe it. In a gas chamber! Olga dear, are you absolutely sure?"

"My dear Rozsi, I only wish I wasn't so sure. Believe me, I have my reasons when I tell you not to expect your mother back."

Mum continued sobbing. Dad buried his head in his palms.

"Mengele was standing there at the gate," Auntie Olga whispered, "and he was selecting people. Your mother went to the right with Erzsike and little Tomi." Erzsike is the wife of Dad's brother and Tomi is my cousin, two years older than me.

"I was sent to the left, my mother to the right. My little Zsuzsi was standing in the middle between us, and I said to her, 'Go with grandma, sweetheart', I sent her to her death! My own child!"

"But how could you have known where she was going?"

"No, I should have stayed with her. Then at least I would be dead too. I don't know anything about my dear Józsi. I might be the only one alive." There was silence. Everybody was weeping.

"They were taken into a room," Auntie Olga continued, "they thought it was a shower room. The guards locked the doors behind them and let the *cyclone B* gas in."

Mum couldn't take any more. She cried out aloud. Dad touched her arm gently. "Darling, the child…"

"As if they were bugs," whispered my mother. "Oh, God… I can't take any more… I just can't…

There was a very long silence. I heard Auntie Olga speak first.

"Any news about your father and about Bandi?" she asked.

Bandi is Dad's older brother.

"We haven't heard anything about Rózsi's father," Dad whispered. "Bandi was seen shot dead by a fellow soldier. He was shot during a decimation." Oh my God! Why would anyone want to shoot Uncle Bandi?

I couldn't go back to sleep for hours. After Auntie Olga had left my parents whispered in the dark for a long time. Then finally I drifted back to my dream world. And now I'm up again. My heart is still thumping loud with fear.

The next morning Mum seems very tired. Her eyes are red from crying. Dad's already left for work. I get up and cuddle up against her. She hugs me close and I feel her shaking. She must have been crying. When I look up at her she smiles faintly at me through her tears and says that after breakfast we'd go down to the out-door swimming pool and do some studying there. We didn't talk. I guess it's easier for her this way. At the pool she gets the reading book out. I don't feel like reading at all. I looked up at her face. She tries to smile but her eyes are horrid. I don't want to make a fuss. My reading is clumsy. She corrects me half-heartedly. Then we go into the pool. I can already do five strokes without help.

It went on like this for a week. In the afternoons I had a nap and then I did some maths with Dad.

One night I woke up with a start. Mum was packing clothes into a sports bag. I shook with fear. "Where are we going now?" I asked in a whisper. She jumped and stopped packing, turned around and walked over to me. She sat down on my bed.

"Sweetheart, Daddy is not feeling well, his heart aches. Aunt Irma has called the ambulance, they'll be here soon. I'll go to the hospital with Daddy. I may not be home before the morning. Aunt Irma will stay here, you won't be alone. Go back to sleep. By the time you wake up, I'll be home."

"And if I hadn't woken up, would you have left without me?"

"Of course not, don't be silly. I would have woken you up before we left."

I heard Dad moan. She stroked my hair one last time.

Then the ambulance arrived and two men came into the room with a stretcher. They lifted up Dad from the bed and over to the stretcher. Then Aunt Irma closed the door and gave out a big sigh.

I looked up at her. I'd never seen her at night before. She was standing there in the dimly lit hallway with curling pins in her hair. Her skinny legs stuck out from under the nightgown. She walked into the kitchen and then returned with a paper bag.

"Take one, Gabika," she said and held the bag in front of me.

I took a candy.

"Thank you."

"Alright now," she put a hand on my head, "go to bed now. Your father will be fine, you'll see."

She waited for me to go back to bed and then I heard her close the door of her room. I stepped inside the empty room. I didn't switch the light off. I ran my fingers across Dad's bed, then across Mum's. I sat on the bed. The window was open. A light breeze came in. I suddenly felt cold so I slipped into Mum's bed. I pulled the duvet over my head. This way I may survive, I thought, in this cave.

I started shivering. I was shivering on that day too. The day of the deportation when they said that the old and the children should sit on the cart on top of the luggage and the adults would follow on foot. We'd meet in one and a half hours. I didn't want to, I didn't want to leave my parents.

3.

The sun was shining brightly, the ride was long. It must have been around noon by the time the cart stopped and rest time was ordered. Some ate some didn't. They didn't give me food because they said we'd meet soon anyway. A grandmother made a jam sandwich for her granddaughter. I shouldn't be watching them, they might think I'm begging, but I just couldn't help staring. The grandmother said, "Come here." She put some jam on a slice of bread and gave it to me. I felt ashamed. I shouldn't have let them know I was so hungry.

We bumped along on the cart all afternoon. At dusk we finally turned into a village, stopped in front of a huge barn and everybody got off. The tractor was disconnected from the cart and went on its way. The cart with all the bags stayed there. I walked into the barn and looked around. There was a big farmyard behind the door and sheds for storing hay all around. The roof was supported by wooden poles. Suddenly I heard a rumbling noise coming towards us. Our group had arrived. Everybody seemed in a hurry. They pulled their bags down from the cart and ran to find a good place for themselves for the night.

My heart sank. My parents and our luggage were nowhere to be seen. We wouldn't have shelter for the night and it would all be my fault.

I ran out to the cart struggling and frantically started looking for our bag. I found it at last. I dragged it off the cart but I couldn't lift it. I started pulling it inside. Hundreds of people ran past me. My legs went suddenly weak. I fell down and started sobbing. Suddenly I heard my mother's voice.

"O, my little sweetheart, we were so worried about you. And I didn't even give you food with you."

"Pataki Agi's grandma gave me a slice of bread with jam."

"God bless her for that, I'll pay her back."

That's when I started shivering. Dad wrapped his coat around me. He put his palm on my forehead.

"Must be at least thirty-eight," he whispered to Mum, "and I don't even have an aspirin. Wait here, I'll try and get one somewhere."

After a short time they made me sit up and take a pill with some water. They kept me warm from both sides.

Suddenly my shivering stopped. I fell asleep.

4.

I stick my head out from under the duvet. The room is familiar. They're our clothes in the wardrobe. We don't have to leave.

The best thing to do is to get all the blankets together. I drag them over to Mum's bed and hide under them. I even cover my head. It's morning soon, and she is coming…

I look out. Mum's sitting at the table, her head in her hands, crying.

She wipes her tears and smiles at me.

"Were you cold last night?"

"I was but I'm alright now. How's Dad?"

"He's in good hands. He has to stay in the hospital for a while. We'll go visit him. I'm going to have a bit of a rest now, alright? There's something to eat on the shelf. Have some breakfast and then read quietly. When I wake up we'll discuss what to do today."

The sun is already high by the time Mum wakes up. We put everything away together and then we go to the market.

Dad had a heart attack last night. He has to rest. Mum can go to see him every day but I can only visit him after a couple of days.

The vendors put their goods out under the shade of the giant trees of the boulevard. There's a separate place for fruit and vegetables, for the diary products, for the pickles and peppers. I know the market well. I used to come here with grandma. The smell of fruit and dill reminds me of the old days.

We pass grandma's house. One side of the gate is open and we can see through the cool, dark gateway the little garden filled with sunshine.

"Let's go inside a bit," I say to Mum, and without waiting for a reply I walk in. Mum says nothing, just follows close behind me.

A couple of low steps lead to grandma's flat from the yard. I was told that when I was learning to walk I'd spent hours climbing up and down those steps. Later, and I remember that well, I used to like sitting there and playing. Sometimes grandma would bring a chair and sit next to the door and tell me stories.

On the stairs there are two children playing I've never seen before. The door is open wide. A young woman wearing a kerchief is putting out the bedding to air on the windowsill. She glances briefly at the children and then disappears.

"Grandma's bed linen," Mum whispers, "and her curtains too..." She can't take her eyes off the window.

I don't dare look at her but I can sense that she's crying.

What if we went over to the woman and asked to have grandma's curtains back? Would she also slam the door in our face? Or would she say: "You should be happy to have come back. Some people just have all the nerve!"

"Let's go," said Mum. She turned to face me and cupped my face in her hands. "We won't see grandma again. She's not coming back."

At last! I knew she expected me to start crying, to be shocked, to ask something. I could feel my face grow stiff, my eyes go blank and words got stuck in my throat. Because I knew more than that.

I met Pista Tausz at the swimming pool. He told me that those who were killed in the gas chambers were then burnt and the smoke was swirling from a big chimney. People were locked up in a camp that was surrounded by electric barbed wire fence. If somebody wanted to escape or just touched the fence accidentally, they died immediately. Pista had overheard the conversation between his Mum and their guests who came back from a camp like that. A mother and her adult daughter had visited them, distant relatives, and they were in the gas chamber as well. Of course they didn't know at the time. Suddenly the first two rows were let out for some reason. Maybe they had to do some work urgently. When they got out a German called over to them.

"Do you know where you have just been? In the gas chamber."

I think about it a lot. It could easily have been me who'd been sent there. And I wouldn't have been let out.

I always wake up at night. I seem to see a burglar climbing up on the stove in the darkness. I'm scared. I have to sleep in the afternoon, too. I don't like it. I always dream too much. And I wake up sweating.

5.

Dad has already been in the hospital for a week when Mum realises that my cheeks are always red when I wake up. She touches my forehead and takes my temperature. She checks for three days. Every afternoon I have a temperature.

On the forth day Mum takes me to see Doctor *Kalocsai,* "Previously *Kohn*," she adds laughing.

The waiting room is full of photographs of the children Doctor *Kalocsai* has treated. My picture is there too, third row from the top, from when I was two. I was quite a nice little boy. My hair is black and curly, like Mum's. The doctor calls us in, asking all about Dad and our flat hunt.

"I noticed three days ago that he has a temperature in the afternoons," Mum says in a slightly shaking voice.

"Let's have a look," smiles the doctor. "Take your shirt off."

He moves his stethoscope over my back and my chest and I shiver.

"Now, step up here, I'll x-ray you."

When I get dressed again he puts his hand on my head and says, "Wait outside for a minute son, will you?"

When Mum comes out she suggests we take a walk in the hospital garden. We sit down on a white bench and I wait.

"Doctor *Kalocsai* had a look at your lungs," she begins, "you know, there are these little bubbles in there and the Doctor says that these bubbles got swollen at one point. It's not a big problem but now you have to rest a lot and you'll get some medicine as well. The best thing is to travel to the mountains to a sanatorium, but I don't you to go away. There's a Jewish children's home just on the outskirts of the city with a big park. The

Doctor knows the doctors over there and will tell them about you. You'll stay there for a couple of weeks in the fresh air. You'll get medication, you won't run around and play, and by the time autumn comes you'll be ready to go to school."

I'm speechless. I have to go again, I have to go alone. Is everybody ill there or am I going to be the only one who has to stay in bed all day?

"Come on, sweetheart, we'll go and see Daddy," she said.

From the wide, well-lit corridor we enter into a hospital room with six beds in it. Dad is lying next to the window. He smiles at us as we enter the room.

"Hello son, I haven't seen you for ages. I hear you're going on a vacation. So how are things? How are you doing with the studying?" Dad looks so strange lying on that white hospital bed. He seems very skinny and his voice sounds strangely different.

"I'm getting better at reading," I manage finally.

"You'll have a lot of time to study now. Practice your maths as well. When I get out of here I'll buy you new books."

We leave Dad and I kiss each other on the cheek. I turn back once more from the door. Dad is smiling and waving at us.

6.

The next morning I leave for the children's home.

The first couple of days seem endlessly long. Then slowly I settle into a daily routine but by that time everything becomes monotonous and boring. It's summertime after all.

Peter Koltai spent a week with me in the infirmary, then a sixteen year old boy came next, and after that others came, always someone else. Sometimes I would be alone in the room for days.

Most of them have no family in the world and they all want to go Palestine. They're all learning Hebrew and mix Hebrew words into their sentences when they talk.

In the evenings they would light a bonfire and dance around it singing loudly, or just sit around the fire and sing Hebrew songs I've never heard before. I can't go and sit with them. I don't really belong here. The fact that I am Jewish and they are Jewish seems insignificant now.

Mum came exactly three times a week to visit me. She'd bring me semolina pudding with fruit and eggs. Every time she came we studied a bit together, she prepared homework for me and checked the ones I'd finished from the previous days. I got colour pencils, a sketchbook, *plasticine* and a colouring book.

The others who stayed at the infirmary would play pick-up-sticks with me if they were not too sick. I asked them why they were going to Palestine. It's our homeland, they'd answer. We'll build it for ourselves and then nobody can persecute us there because we'll defend ourselves. How, I asked? With weapons, of course. Jews with weapons? I liked the idea.

"Please, can we go to Palestine, too?" I asked Mum.

She was surprised.

"We can't go there," she answered after hesitating for a while.

"Why? Aren't we Jewish?"

"Yes, we are unfortunately," she said with a bitter smile. "But, you know, Palestine is a very very poor country. It's extremely hot over there all year round. Almost the whole place is a desert."

"But everybody is going there. They don't think it's a desert."

"What would we live on? We're not young any more. Dad's got a job here and we'll have our own flat soon. We can't just leave for the unknown."

"What if they want to hurt us again over here?"

"They can't hurt us now. The Russians are here now."

"What if they weren't here?"

"Look, sweetheart, people are not bad. There was a smaller group of people who didn't like us, so they did a lot of bad things to us. These people are now facing the courts and they will be punished."

"What about the Germans?"

"They lost the war. They'll never ever be the same as they were in the past."

I wasn't convinced. I would have liked to leave. It would have been much better far away from here. We weren't safe here. Anything could happen here.

At night, in the dark, I was left alone with the dead. They were suffocating me. They ran into the electric fence and died, heavy smoke came swirling out of a huge chimney. And in the day they were with me too. They were shouting at me, scolding me, arguing with me. I tried to defend myself but there were too many of them.

What have I done to deserve to stay alive? Where is everybody? Is it because we weren't loved? Is it a reason for killing someone? I don't really like Aunt Irma, so can I kill her? Why grandma and Toni? Who were they bothering? Who was I bothering that I could get tossed around for a year and have all my toys taken away? Why did all this happen? Nobody answered my questions.

So do *I* have to answer them? Me? I'm only just learning to read and I'm left here alone, sitting between walls of silence with my dead and with my thoughts. Why can't they read my mind? Why don't they answer? Do they not know themselves? The adults, who know everything? They turn their eyes away from the horrors. They do not look. My eyes don't ask if they can look or not. The dead are there always and everywhere. I cannot send them away. They are calling me, they are shouting at me. You are one of us! You belong here with us! Why didn't you come with us? Do you think you are different?

I try to defend myself. No, I am not different. It's just an accident. Please forgive me. I can't help being alive, don't be angry with me, please. I will die eventually when I get old.

But we died young, they scream. And your mother doesn't even feel pity for us. There aren't enough students in the school, that's what she says. And why is *she* alive? There are all these orphans here. None of them has a mother and yours is alive. It's not fair!

Leave me alone, leave me alone, I beg them. I want to wake up. It's a dream. It's not a dream.

This is reality! Face it!

I can't face it. It's killing me, I'm going to die, too. You'll take me with you, I know.

I'm scared, I'm scared! I don't understand. Maybe we did something terrible, only I don't know about it. There must be a reason for this horror, surely. There must be something dark lurking somewhere behind it all.

If we weren't guilty, how could Mum just say that there aren't enough students in the school? Just like that, as simple as that. Surely, she knows something that I don't know.

She knows there's nothing to shout about because they were right. We deserved to be punished.

But what have *I* done? Or do I and all other children have to suffer the consequences of the sins of the adults? Oh, how I hate the sinners who caused us all this trouble! How I hate the Jews! No, no! I don't want to be Jewish any more.

You don't *want* to be? But you *are*! The dead are shouting.

No! If I want, I won't be a Jew any more. No, no, no! I can't take it any more!

If I'm not Jewish any more, I can forget about you. I don't belong with you. I'm not responsible for you.

The dead slowly withdrew to a distant little chamber of my soul and I slowly closed the door behind them. They disappeared. My heart, however, grew heavier and heavier. And threateningly and unpredictably the world began to tower above my head.

Translation by Ágnes Lánczos

Szöllős Vera

Szöllős Vera was born in 1937 in Szeged, Hungary, into a totally assimilated Jewish family. In 1944, when she was seven years old, together with her family, she was deported to Czechoslovakia. Here, she and her family survived the war and the Holocaust, under rather difficult circumstances but in relative safety. In 1950 with her family she moved to Budapest and lives there till today.

She married, has two children and three grandchildren.

In her mature years she began to write mainly life-like stories and biographies.

Anna Kun

COMING HOME

I'm trudging along Kossuth Utca all the way from the station to the city centre, desperate, in a pair of jeans cut short, boots, blue linen shirt, carrying a German military calfskin backpack. It's a small bag and it opens like those leather tobacco pouches with overlapping sides. Only a few things fit into it but other stuff can also be packed under the big brown and white spotted hairy flaps, like coats or blankets. My hair's short, boyishly cropped. It's early summer, quiet and peaceful. Only in my soul, storms are raging.

I decided to leave on my own. My father and mother stayed on in Budapest at the religious community center where they were receiving aid: some advice or a loan to start over again. There were masses of others waiting with them. I grew restless though, couldn't stay any longer. I wanted to know if Pista was really at home. I didn't want anyone else to be there when the two of us met again. I had to see what the war had destroyed in us, how we were to live on after all this. Was he expecting me to come home? Did he guard my memory within himself as I did his? Is it possible to start everything all over again? We'd hardly lived together, what did we know about one another?

Is it still possible to live in this city? Is it possible to stay here where I was last seen with a bundle on my back, in someone else's coat, together with a bunch of frightened women, old men and children, stumbling towards the station, driven on by yelling military police and Arrow-Cross men? Here, where everyone knew me but nobody could or would do a thing for me. Would their shame and my shame allow me to live here again?

I walk along with my head hung low, I'm ashamed to have come back, I'm ashamed to be alive. I don't want anyone to recognize me, I don't want anyone to greet me, to stop me, to ask me questions. *I* was ashamed that the city had looked so silently upon our being driven away, and now it would have to take some of us back. We would be an incarnation of its guilt. And some could not yet accept the idea that there might be survivors they would have to face.

In the calfskin bag there's almost nothing. A change of underwear, a temporary identity card I was given in Budapest. All that I have now I paid for last year. This story I'm carrying with me weighs down terribly on my shoulders. My knees buckle under its weight. I see all those images in spite of myself, they are burnt into my retina. There's that night in Bergen-Belsen in the diphtheria barracks where the Dutch surgeon was operating on the Greek woman, in vain. Spectators all around, the other patients crouching, wrapped in blankets on the triple bunk beds. Rain was beating against the roof and gathering in pools on the barrack floor. The doctor was operating by candlelight, his stout, stooping figure a shadow on the wall grown huge. I see him spread his arms and stand by the table, crushed. I see the woman's face white as wax, slowly disappear under the coarse blanket being pulled over her. And I see myself a year earlier, before leaving the ghetto, trying on that brown winter coat which almost reached the ground and thinking that would suit me fine. I put that dark shawl on my head. Not even my mother would have known me. And I see the five litre bottle of honey on the garden table, knocked over, someone had hastily propped his backpack against it before leaving... honey was dripping lazily, spilling in sparkling golden streams in the dazzling sunlight. And I see my little son on the examination table, wasted to skin and bone, eyes wide open with terror, his mouth curved to cry, not wanting to lie down, reaching towards me...

It's early in the afternoon with almost no traffic around. Two men are just rounding the corner at the grammar school, talking. They're quite close now, and there's something about the voice... I look up. My heart misses a beat. I have to lean on the fence. It's Pista. I have wanted to stay alive for this very moment. The hope of this moment got me through typhoid, through fever. Also the knowledge that I've got something to do in this world, to set things right. But what it is I've got to do is left for Pista to decide, he knows.

Did we embrace one another? Did we hold hands? Was there joy and fulfillment in finding one another? I don't know. I was out of my wits. I'd arrived home.

"Meet the mayor, my friend," he said. "Tibor, this is my wife. We're going home now. We'll carry on tomorrow, okay?" he told him. Then he asked, "The boy?" I waved him silent with a single motion.

He took my hand and we walked on side by side. Without a word. A block further he asked again.

"I couldn't bring him home. He's not alive."

He let my hand go. I felt he wasn't happy to see me. He'd expected the child home more than me. We went to our old house. I put the backpack down on the porch, stumbled over it and such a fit of crying burst out of me that I almost died. Pista startled sat down beside me and patted my back.

"Try to forget! Don't look back! It will pass. You'll forget...We're here, we've got plenty to do."

I've been trying ever since to forget. I never talked about what I'd been through.

A bare yard had taken the place of our old garden. Old tires thrown about, wheel tracks in the mud. The pines and bushes were no more. We lived in a strange house, among strange furniture, in a small, strange room. Gone was our home. Gone was our youth.

Nothing was ever going to be like it was.

Translation by Ágnes Merényi

Anna Kun

Anna Kun was born in 1920 into a lower-middle class family in the Hungarian countryside. Before the war she worked as a beautician, a nurse, a weaver and in the leather industry. In 1944 she was deported together with her four month old baby from the Szeged brick factory to Austria where she worked in a munitions factory for six months. Then she was deported to Bergen-Belsen, a concentration camp in Germany. Finally she was liberated in Terezin, a Czechoslovakian concentration camp. After 1945 she became a journalist and an editor of children's magazines (Pajtas, Pioneer and the Slovakian Nas Pajtas). She also worked for the radio program Iskola Radio (School Radio). She holds a university degree in pedagogy. She is the mother of two children. This story is part of a longer series of recollections which she presented chapter by chapter to her daughter Vera Suranyi. Anna Kun died in 2005.

Anna Szász

VARIATIONS ON A FATHER
(Excerpts from a memoir)

Key words:
He died
Farewell
Waiting for a…

*

"You father?"
Ilse F., my classmate in elementary school, and her mother, addressed me in the early summer of 1947, on the corner of V. Street and the boulevard. I was just going to the swimming pool, the Indoor, as we used to call it. A cruel winter was just been behind me, with claustrophobia, depression, fights with my younger brother, puberty; my breasts had begun to grow: "Hey, Romola, yours cables have grown", and his plump forefinger pointed at me with a derisive smile, and I jumped at him, although I knew that he had become stronger than me. This inconvenient part of my body was bothering me, it ached and tightened, my arms rubbed against it, which at the same time caused me some hidden pleasure, too, but this only exacerbated the chaos in me. But at that moment it was all behind me, nothing else mattered than being out there as soon as possible, out in the sun, in the water, and amongst the boys, which I concealed even from myself: and then Ilse came with her mother.

"Your father?"

„He died!"

I didn't say what we usually did, „He did not come back", which left a rift, some kind of a chance for those who inquired. No! I used the definite statement. The irreversible one. Stating the unadornable fact.

"He died?"

They both threw up their hands in astonishment. They resembled each other. They had longish, thick heads, and they were both rather stocky, they looked more like sisters than mother and daughter, and they behaved as if my father's death had been an individual, chance accident.

"Yes, he died."

And I had to laugh.

I could see the shock, the indignation on their faces.

I was laughing, laughing, laughing.

I was laughing...

*

...I couldn't identify the places of those years, the houses, the streets. The names of places gained a special significance. Isaszeg, Felsőgalla and Cegléd, the stations of my father's first term of forced labor service are not regular human settlements in my imagination. Gödöllő. It does not signify a castle, the park, a village that has grown into a town by this time, but a sinister, ominous name for me. The place from which they were taken to Ukraine, in September 1941. A Sunday in early autumn, a closed, grass-covered area, where the labor servicemen and their families could meet and say good-bye. The air was warm and full of dust. I could have thought it was almost like an excursion, as we sat on the grass, and my mother unpacked the food she had brought from home, and she must have brought something to drink, too, and perhaps some coffee for the two of them in a thermos. If I had been able to formulate then what it means to be forced to be somewhere, nailed down, as if one had been withdrawing from oneself as time passes. And the things that surround one get more and more unreal, floating, drifting. But I was only eight years old, and a child cannot think in such a complex manner. I was only exhausted, bored, and as always, I got anxious when I heard commands. My father jumped up and lined up with the others, and then suddenly there was a hitherto invisible wire fence between us.

...(To be waiting for a father.)

After Tessza, B.'s piano teacher called me and told me that we could buy an old piano from the school (how did she know about our financial situation?) I stood in front of the piano room at 8 a.m. the very next morning.

I should have realised they opened at 10.

I was carried away by enthusiasm.

Alas!

Yes, alas. An enthusiasm to get this piano for my daughter, an instrument that turned out to be inconvenient later. It was huge, with a wooden soundboard, later I couldn't sell it. No one wanted it, even for free. By then B. had already moved away from home. She didn't care about the chaffinches her father brought home either. These birds that lived on the piano, scattering seeds and their feathers all over, are symbols of disorder in my eyes. Nothing is in order. (Time is out of joint: O cursed spite.) Nothing.

I stood there, as if I thought that waiting matters.

It would be a great deed if I managed to get the piano for B.

As if things could be remedied backwards.

We hadn't had a piano at home.

This, like so many other things, were missing from the requisites of bourgeois existence.

"A meek girl is walking in the streets."

Someone, I don't remember who, a woman, not a relative, used to play such vaudeville songs on the piano, in my aunt E.'s drawing room, where the furniture was covered with violet velvet.

That drawing room – or was it perhaps cyclamen?

("The sunshine gets brighter on her cheeks."

This is it.

I've got it.

"And as she is waddling and striding away,

A nice gentleman is coming her way.")

Early in the morning.

The piano room was only a few steps away from the corner of the boulevard and the narrow street of the hospital (it is called City Sanatorium now) where my first abortion was done by Dr. I. H., who was gentle in spite of the rough appliances used at that time. He called me darling, and ensured me that I should not think of myself as a girl who got into trouble – one and a half corners away from the Nyugati railway station.

Two steps forward, two steps back. There's hardly any traffic, only a few men and women are hurrying to work.

Waiting – it is a continuous activity, connecting the past and the present.

No!

It is a state of existence.

I am standing in front of the Nyugati railway station.

A train is arriving. A crowd. People are flocking outside. But then fewer and fewer people come, and there are only one or two late passangers left in the end.

I am still waiting.

Another train, another crowd, more hope. Perhaps. And then no again.

The sun is going down, the shadows are getting longer. I am only held there by the inertia of helplessness. I feel ashamed of waiting there every day, in front of the Nyugati, all through the summer and early autumn following the war – it's my secret.

Deep inside I feel that what I'm doing is a violation of the law I don't know which one, but it must exist.

A feeling flashes inside me, suddenly: what if we have missed each other?

What if he gets home while I'm waiting?

He arrived once, unexpectedly, so why couldn't it happen again?

I see him appearing in the corridor, wearing an army uniform without a collar, a soldier's cap, holding my younger brother who had no idea who this stranger was. My mother was cleaning, wearing her beige dressing gown with a red and while polka-dotted shawl on her head. The doorbell rings, she opens the door.

When my father hugs me, I feel that characteristic male smell, a mixture of odors from his body, tobacco and heavy iron. He travelled home from Ukraine on a freight train.

It was strange to get used to that male smell in the apartment full of women's and children's smells.

My father smokes a pipe. He whistles while he is shaving. Life is more eventful after he gets home. Men come to visit us, men who are younger than him, his mates and women who belong to them. Laci P. and Lili H. – they were the most beautiful couple I have ever seen, not on film but in reality.

My father and my mother are dancing. A 41 year old man and a 35 year old woman, who had been separated for 25 months. Letters, parcels, army postcards. My mother did not cover her head during the unusually cold winter of 1941-42, at –15 °C, when knee-deep snow covered the streets of the city, to show her solidarity with my father. She got ill, tormented by sinusitis for weeks. Now they are dancing. I am disturbed by the modest, but still perceptible eroticism between them. I feel uncomfortable.

My father takes me to ski.

To visit exhibitions.

Gets me an English teacher.

He is planning to buy me a piano accordion...

There's some movement behing the glass portal.

The piano room is being opened.

My waiting has ended.

(No! I could never stop waiting.)

This is the first time it occurs to me that this *me*, who I am, was formed as a consequence of my father's death. Had he stayed alive, had he come back, nothing would have happened in the same way; then there would be another me, a stranger, an unknown self, who doesn't have much to do with my current self.

Thirty years after his death, I killed my father...

Translation by Ágnes Merényi

Anna Szász

Anna Szász was born in 1933 in Budapest, into a middle-class bourgeois Jewish family. She survived the Holocaust in Budapest. Her father died in a forced labor camp in Buchenwald. She finished her studies at the Eötvös Loránd University in Budapest in 1956. She became a chemist. She worked as an engineer in a textile factory, then she became a journalist in 1969. For 5 or 6 years she worked for factory journals, then for Nők Lapja (Women's Magazine), from 1975 till 1992, when she retired. During these years she also wrote for many other magazines and for the Civil Radio.

She has two adult children and three grandsons.

Vera Meisels

SALTY COFFEE

A long time ago, when I was still married to the Israeli-born father of my two wonderful children, we lived in a warm and pleasant home. We could relax and talk about many things, among which the plastic arts and music were prominent. Music lovers came to us to listen to records played on the sophisticated sound system that had been my husband's lifelong dream, a dream I had been able to fulfill when I received reparations for my persecution by the Nazis.

We met at the Avni Art School and I fell truly in love with him. His charm was enhanced by the uniform of the Israeli Air Force, in which he was a career officer. In addition, he was a gifted sculptor and could whistle Bach suites without a false note.

Subsequently, a psychologist explained to me that my enthusiasm over his talents and my admiration for his potential were unfounded. "*Unrealized potential is impotence!*" said she. I paid for the session, but regretted that the information had come twenty years too late.

When we had guests, I was in charge of cakes and biscuits, while my husband was master of ceremonies and in charge of liquid refreshments, mainly tea and coffee. Since I was born in Czechoslovakia, the cakes were naturally Central European in flavor. My mother imparted an important secret to me: "*Remember, what goes in is what comes out. If you use margarine instead of butter, it's a fake!*" To this day, our guests remember the fragrance and taste of those plum and apricot cakes. One summer evening, when the children were in bed, we were serving coffee and cake to two couples we had invited to our home. I was in the kitchen, attending to the apricot cake and my husband was in the sitting room amusing the guests. When I came in with the cake, he asked them who wanted tea and who wanted coffee; he knew that I always had strong instant coffee with a drop of milk.

I chatted with our guests until my husband entered with the laden tray. I took a sip from my cup, only to discover that my coffee was extremely salty. However, I drank it without saying anything. Our guests watched me in amazement. Finally, one of them gathered the courage to ask, "Wasn't your coffee salty?"

"And how! But to tell the truth," I said, " it had its advantages and I enjoyed it."

"How's that possible? Why didn't you tell him?" she persisted.

I wasn't sure how to phrase my answer, After all, they were all proud *sabras*, whereas I had only earned the right to be defined by the term that was my husband's original invention: "*Holocaustnik*". (My computer program for correct spelling does not recognize the word! In fact, most people do not know how to interpret this nickname and I must admit that it also took me a long time to lift my head and feet and get myself all the way to the divorce court.)

I was not sure whether to give my guests an honest explanation for my enjoyment of the coffee, or simply change the subject. At last, I decided that having been asked, I may as well reply. Particularly since my listeners seemed to be attentive and empathetic. I didn't know that my husband had planned to entertain them at my expense, nor that he had bet them that I would drink the coffee with salt, because I wasn't choosy about food, or anything else, and I could eat whatever came on my way. They did not believe him and lost the bet. He crowed in triumph, one word led to another and the incident took an unexpected turn.

"Listen, my friends," I said, "I've never told you about the hunger I experienced in the trench. We lay there in the mountains like mummies, dug into a pit that was only deep enough to take us lying down, with an army canvas pressing on us because of the weight of the snow that was also good camouflage. For the first few days, we had some food, a bit of bread, a bit of sausage and cubes of sugar our parents managed to stuff into the knapsacks when we escaped from the '*actions*' that were supposed to wipe us out. We lay like that throughout the days and crawled out only at night to stretch our limbs and eat, if you could call it that, when the Germans and their dogs stopped patrolling the forest in search of Jews and partisans. At first, we ate the food we brought with us. Later, Mother melted snow over a candle and added leaves and pine cones to make a warm drink for us.

"I honestly don't want to burden you with stories my husband calls the product of my sick imagination as a Holocaustnik. He claims that the real hunger and horror took place in Jerusalem, during the siege, when the suffering was seven times worse. The grocery stores were shut for days on end! The supply of milk products was irregular. His family had to eat halva and all sorts of things they had in the larder! At times the taps stopped running and they had to carry it in buckets from the distribution points!"

I felt a little sorry for the guests and wondered why I washing our dirty linen in public. But, to be frank, I felt I could lean on them. They were stunned, they wanted to hear more and more, while my husband sat as silent as a fish. When he did try to put in a word, or change the subject, they almost crudely silenced him.

"Yes, go on," they urged me, "and how does the salty coffee come into it?"

"It comes in, I assure you!" I said. "You see, first of all, I enjoyed the coffee because my husband made it for me, which is in itself a treat. It may also be seen in a positive light, we could decide that he made a mistake and used salt instead of sugar. And why shame him in front of you? Anyway, where's it written that coffee must be sweet and not salty? It was hot and strong. Believe me, even as a child I'd have been happy to get such coffee instead of melted snow! Things must be kept in proportion! This applies to food as well. Take it from me, I'm not a bin that accepts any rubbish, but I'm also not in a hurry to throw something out just because the date has expired, as long as it still smells fresh. And it's true that I don't feel the need to eat in fancy restaurants.

"Whenever I buy meat for the hamburgers the children and I love, I have to face an interrogation from him: 'Did you insist that they wash the mince-machine? Have you heard of salmonella?'"

At this point he started to lecture the guests on the dangers of germs and the rate at which they multiply, but one of the men shouted at him, "Enough! Let her talk, we've heard enough from you!"

The coffee incident took place in the 'seventies, meaning that those friends had known me for almost twenty years. Until that day, I had never told them about myself, because, in fact, I never had a chance. My husband always controlled the conversation. That evening, he, the director of the salty coffee joke, ended up shamed and even rejected. When I saw our guests to the door, he remained sitting in the living room. I was warmed by the hugs from my friends as they left. "*Be strong!*", they said.

I was living in a bubble of illusions when I built myself a model of successful partnership. To me, the integration between a new immigrant and a native Israeli seemed to be the recipe for us to have children who would grow up without the 'second generation' syndrome. Children healthy in spirit and proud of Israel.

My friends must have known that divorce lay ahead of me, but I waited for a number of years after that evening, until the children were older, before I again dared to liberate myself.

Translation from Hebrew by Riva Rubin

Vera Meisels

Vera Meisels was born in Czechoslovakia, on June 11, 1936, into a Slovakian-Hungarian Jewish family. Her family was arrested by the Germans and taken to Sered, a Slovak Internment Camp. In December 1944, she, her mother and her sister were taken to Theresienstadt, via Auschwitz. After the liberation she left for Israel with a Zionist youth group, and lived on a Kibbutz. There she stayed for seven years, then she left for Tel Aviv to study art and also embarked on a career at a bank. Eventually, she became a branch vice-president. She publishes poems and short stories in English, in Slovak and in Hungarian.

Miriam Ben-David

THE CASE OF A BIZARRE DREAM

September 1998. A sultry autumn day. We are meeting at Ludd Airport. Ronnie, my oldest son, the father of four, Gila, my daughter, who committed her four children to the care of her husband, and Uriel Binyamin, who I used to jokingly call Benjamin Oedipus when he was a child, now the father of three kids – all of them are waiting there for me.

"What a strange feeling, to be traveling like this, as if we were children again," Gila says.

I'm very much upset. I'm afraid that they're going to be disappointed. I feel guilty for separating these busy people from their families, their work, to accompany me on this "roots tour", which is so fashionable now in Israel.

We're going to celebrate my birthday, here, where I was born, a place from which I was ripped out without any preparation.

But what do they have to do with it?

It's very important for me that they meet the Christian family that hid us, those who risked their lives for us. Even if it was not them who saved my life in the end, but our illegal flight across the border to Romania. But that does not detract from their merit, of course.

This is not the first time I'm going to meet them. We haven't lost touch throughout the last 54 years. I have visited Ági, the daughter who is of the same age as me, the only one of the children to whom her parents revealed the secret. They told her that I was a Jewish girl, not a relative of their aunt from the country, a few years ago, when I attended a conference in Budapest. We were both widowed in that year. I've also met Imre once. He read out parts of his diary later, and it turned out that he made every effort to cheer me up during those sad days of my staying with them. I met Zoló, who used to be a very attentive and naughty nine-year-old boy, in 1979, when their mother was still alive, and brought us all together in the old family home. Zoló told me then that he was wondering why I never spoke about my experiences with his family. He found this very peculiar.

For me this "excursion" is staggering. This is the corner of my world to which only I have access. How can I know what my children may feel? Will I be able to communicate my past experiences to them? I would like my children to know the most significant events of my story, and the people who risked their lives to save mine. I would like to show them the places that filled my childhood with colors, to visit the streets, the buildings and the shops with them, and to share with them the million associations I attach to these images. How can I make what is mine meaningful to them?

Or how can I translate my childhood experiences, the horrors of the Shoah, and the moral consequences drawn from these, into an intelligible and sensible language, for others and myself?

Really, how long have I been dealing with questions related to the Shoah? I don't know.

So far it's been 54 years.

It's true that I have been intrigued for a while. I am curious to know those who were able to risk their lives to save Jewish people, and why. Relatively few researchers deal with this question. I could not find satisfying answers in the dedicated literature either. But I still feel that there must have been something, perhaps not even consciously, in the families that were able to do this, even if their actions were a matter of mere chance, as sometimes happened. And another question: What did their children know and feel? And what is their grandchildren's view on the matter?

I thought I would be able to find some answers visiting "my family".

I'm here with them again. We arranged this birthday meeting via correspondence. Twenty of us are sitting around the table. The children of the family that saved us – my generation – their grandchildren – my children's generation – my three children and myself. It is awesome for me, but at the same time there is something reassuring. I feel as if I was moving in a new sphere, in which I haven't been before. I am filled with curiosity. The air is intoxicating.

Everyone has arrived. Three of the four "children" (the fourth of them, Zoló's twin sister has died recently), the grandchildren, good-looking young people, some of them with their partners, and I, are sitting around the table. Many of the grandchildren speak English very well, and my children also speak Hungarian, although it's somewhat broken. The food is delicious, we all chat merrily, it is as if it was a family reunion.

After dinner, I ask them to talk about their family, so that I can get to know them better, and I also ask what their grandparents told them about their heroic deeds during the time of the Shoah.

But they remain silent. They never talked about this subject. Suddenly Ági stands up, she wants to say something. "You, Miriam, were different from the others. You remembered us. You sent letters and Christmas gifts throughout all these years, while others just disappeared, and turned their back on those who had helped them, ungratefully." I am shocked to hear this, and I feel that the vague feeling I became conscious of on the bank of Lake *Kineret* on that hot summer evening is getting clearer and clearer.

It had happened only a few moths before. I sat all day at a conference, where we were discussing dreams and their interpretations. When my turn came, I related how I had been throwing out huge pieces of frozen meat from a refrigerator during the first part of my dream, looking for a certain piece, while in the second part I was walking in Budapest with a childhood girlfriend. While we were discussing the dream, I realized that I was actually talking about the questions related to my planned "roots tour". Something stirred inside me, and by the time the sun went down, I clearly felt that the planned "tour" would not be without any significance. I was sitting quietly on the bank of the lake, in the darkness, only the moon was shimmering. I didn't know what to do with this message yet, but I knew that I wanted to do something positive, something that would be a record of my memories of the Holocaust, and the conclusions that could be drawn from them. I thought that the best starting point could be the inclusion of those who saved lives into the historical record. I feel that it is important to show appreciation and gratitude to those who broke ranks with the indifferent, and I thought that their behavior, and the moral and social standpoints that stem from it, could be rich soil for developing and promoting anti-racist ideas and projects.

During the time between the conference and our traveling I did my best to find out things, partly in the literature of the Holocaust, about the subject of those who saved people: their roles, motivations; and I also renewed my knowledge about the psychosocial theory of group discussions.

I was thinking of organizing discussion groups, bringing together survivors and people who saved others.

During my stay in Budapest the plans of "Dialogue for Tolerance" became clearer and clearer. I managed to realize my plans, and the program has kept me occupied for six years.

Since then, I spend a month in Hungary twice a year. I have made several interesting, good friends. I have relearned my mother tongue, and I revel in writing my lectures in Hungarian, even if they have many mistakes (which I am always kindly forgiven.)

I don't know what the future brings, as the generation shaping the program will disappear, but for me and for all those who manage to deal with their Holocaust experiences through this, a circle is coming full.

The program called "Dialogue for Tolerance" consists of two parts. We organize ongoing group discussions for first and second generation survivors and rescuers, led by psychologists. Besides this, we organize conferences twice a year, at which experts clarify the history of the Holocaust and the social lessons drawn from it from different standpoints. One aim of the program is the expression and recording of appreciation and gratitude towards the rescuers. It deals with the traumas of survivors and rescuers: still many Jewish people have identity problems because of their experiences during the Holocaust. Most of the program concentrates on education, to use this historical example to direct the thinking of young people against social prejudices and racism.

Miriam Ben-David (Sternberg)
took refuge in Romania in the summer of 1944, when she was 15 years old. She arrived to Palestine in August 1944. After finishing her studies, she began to work as a clinical psychologist. During the last years of her professional activities, she joined the working community of AMCHA, the National Israeli Center for Psychosocial Support of Survivors of the Holocaust and the Second Generation.

Anna Aczél

A LETTER

I don't really like writing, especially about personal matters, so I was very surprised when I felt a stronger and stronger urge to keep and publicize something of the letter I found by accident. I, of course, discussed it with my sibling: the two of us constitute our family now.

The antecedents:

We were one of the families that didn't talk about our Jewish origins after the war. My grandparents would probably have wanted to talk about this, but they respected our parents' wish. They trusted and believed that anti-Semitism would disappear if Jewish people could be regarded as Hungarians, i.e. if we don't stand out. My father, who died in the 1990s, eventually began to see it in a different light. He accepted that his grandchild visited a *kibbutz*, but he didn't live to see that two of his granddaughters live in Israel now, with different identities.

It is characteristic of my mother's coy, shy life that she didn't leave anything personal behind: neither letters nor any papers. I don't know whether it was she herself who destroyed such things, or if she asked my father to do it. Because of this, when I looked at the letter I found in my grandparents' letter bag, I thought it belonged to my grandmother. I know it was not nice of me but, in fact, I did not read it for a long time. 1982, '84, '86 – these are the years my grandmother, grandfather and my mother died, one after the other.

Well, once I began to read it, I was shocked when I saw that it was a letter written by my mother. She probably never sent it, and my grandmother kept it. I don't think that the entire letter would be of interest to others, but parts of it, means a lot to us. Listening to the *Esztertáska* stories, I thought that it might say something not only to us, but also to those who would like to know what life was like for ordinary people. My mother was 22 *then.* Her parents let her marry a young man when she was 16, because they thought the war was coming, so at least she should have something good happening in her life. Otherwise, how could the daughter of a well-known lawyer marry a stonemason? Of course, the well-known lawyer had to emigrate for a while in 1919, as everyone knew he was a social democrat; and the 22 year old stonemason was just as well-read as a university student: an open-minded, inquiring young man, who was befriended by poets and artists alike. I think that the plump, bespectacled girl was enchanted by this beautiful and smart young man and by the romantic nature of their relationship – and he was enchanted by the knowledge that he might be the safeguard of the daughter of such a family. But who knows? During the war, my father mostly lived illegally: he was hiding, or hid others while wearing a Nazi uniform. He helped whomever he could to escape, the members of his family among them. The letter I found was written after all these events were over, to a sibling of my grandmother who lived in America.

I added a few sentences, marked by italics, to the letter, to help others understand it. Most of the people who are mentioned have died – I carefully left out the names of those who are alive.

Dear Feri and Bella!

You complained about not knowing what happened to the family from the time the Germans came in until now. I am trying here to give you an account.

1. Grandpa's family. Pali and Géza were taken away for forced labor service (this was in the end October 1944, when all the men were taken away from the Jewish houses in the ghetto). Pali got a good position: he became an enlisting doctor on the draft board in one of the barracks. Gyuri (Aczél) managed to get Swiss *Schutzpasses* (safe ID cards) for them (Pali, Géza and Márton): that's how they got into that barrack, and Pali could have discharged all of them. (*My grandmother had 9 siblings: Géza, Márton, Pali and Feri, to whom the letter was written, were also her brothers. Pali was a doctor, who didn't leave the people in the camp even when he had*

the chance to leave.) Géza was already in a bad state, he could hardly see, but Pali thought it was better for them to stay in a protected company (this means a company of those with *Schutzpasses* – they thought they would do better), and if the war had ended somewhat sooner, they would have survived. But it lasted too long, and finally they took even the protected units to Germany. It was Klári Bíró's brother-in-law who met them last in Oranienburg, in December. He says that Géza was in a bad state, he was taken to a hospital. Pali was in excellent condition, and everyone liked him a lot. We haven't heard anything definite since then. We received vague, bad news about Pali, but we haven't met anyone who had seen him personally. (The news said that he tried to help someone while marching, and he was shot dead.) Grandpa was in the ghetto, and as soon as the city was liberated, he appeared at Lia's. From there he went to Lili, and from her to Mom, and finally he moved home. His loving daughters agreed with Margit T. that she would move in to keep house for him but Grandpa did not like the idea at all. He found a much prettier and younger woman, and sacked Margit. He still spends his days in cafés, and to make his life more interesting, he keeps arguing with either Uncle Poldi or Uncle Jenő and doing some shady business with infamous lawyers in Budapest.

2. Márton and family: (*Márton was also a brother, whose wife Lia was Christian, and who made sacrifices to help then and later, too. Their son went to Israel, and became a hero there, although he had some problems related to defining whether he was Jewish or not*). Márton also walked in on the same day, when the men were taken away, but Lia got him out, partly with a Schutzpass, and partly as a spouse of an Aryan person, and she hid him at home. No one knows what Marton does exactly: it is just as it had been before, although it is even more curious, but it seems he does it well, as Lia does not even have to work any more. (*This lasted for minutes only, as by the time I got to know Lia, she worked constantly: she sewed for the whole family, put her daughter through medical school, and she was always so kind.*)

3. The Rózsas: Ernő managed to survive it somehow, but he was interned right at the start of the new regime, I think it was after the liberation, and we haven't heard about him recently. Pali was deported from Újpest (*this*

is another Pali, not the doctor mentioned above), but he was taken to Sárvár only: he kept saying that he was the spouse of an Aryan person, and he was allowed to go home. (*The letter gets unclear at this point: the pencil-written lines have been written over by someone, so it is not possible to follow through.*) The Rózsas pulled through in a Swedish protected house, and they are doing very well now.

4. The K.-s: Klari was in a convent for women, and Gyuri in a convent for men, and they felt so good that they still live there, even after the liberation – not separately, of course: Gyuri moved in with Klári, they are living together. Their old apartment was bombed, and their new place is just being finished. They didn't like the old one, anyway, and according to the experts their new apartment will be wonderful, combining all the achievements of modern interior furnishing. Needless to say: Gyuri is doing better than ever.

5. The Kepes family: when they assigned houses for the Jews, neither ours, nor Mom's house was marked Jewish (Mom's house was taken over and used by the Luftwaffe, so they had moved in with us by that time), and we went to live with the Kepes family. As the summer went on, things got easier, we didn't wear the star, neither did Ági and Pali Kepes, we got our apartment back, and we left them. Pali K. had a heart attack because of the constant agitation. He was ill for a long time, and he became completely deaf. Ági's husband was taken away for forced labor service. Jancsi worked at the Portuguese embassy, and when they had to leave the house, he took Ági to the Ritz, where the officers of the embassy lived. Uncle Pali moved into a Portuguese protected house. Ági gave birth to a child right at the beginning of the fight for Budapest, during Christmas, but the hospital was hit by a bomb on the third day, and they sent Ági and the child away. She went to Lia, but the child died there; it died of hunger. But at least her husband was among the first to arrive in the spring (three weeks later). They are well, although Uncle Pali is not as successful as he used to be, as people are stupid, and they don't want to go to a deaf ear specialist; but Ági's husband makes a good living. To show how time passes I tell you that Jancsi K. is finishing high school this year: he is very clever and talented, he will presumably become a doctor. (*He did become a doctor, he*

is a recognized oncologist in America. We met him in 1986, right before our mother died: he was lecturing at a conference for oncologists. Mother was very ill at that time, so I don't remember our meeting too well.)

6. Lili and the others: I am not writing about them, as Lili has related everything in the letter she sent with Bandi, Dezső H.'s son. Mari is also finishing high school, she is very nice and pretty. She would like to become a hotel manager, and we would support her, but this profession has no future here at the moment. I am afraid that her talent will be lost.

7. Mom and us: The German occupation was like a bolt from the not so blue sky. We knew that this would happen in all probability before the end of the war, but we hoped it would not be so early. We suspected that they would have enough time to finish their job here before the Russians finished them off. At first I felt incredibly angry at the thought that I would not live till the end of it. By that time we knew exactly what had happened to the Yugoslavian, Slovakian and Polish Jews, and we had no reason to believe that we'd survive. Then they began to intern the Jewish lawyers, according to lists put together by Nazi lawyers. I think they got to the letter D, and then stopped. Father was probably saved by his eminently Christian-sounding name. But anyway, for a long time we kept his luggage packed out in the hall, so that he would not have to hurry if he had to go. He got fifty phone calls every evening from people asking how he was. Then they switched off the telephones of the Jewish people, except for the doctors, so this form of amusement ended, too. Everybody was paralyzed in the head at that time. Nobody thought of ways to escape illegally, they just went to the slaughterhouse obediently. Then we had to begin to wear the yellow star. I cannot say what it was like, what we felt when we had to walk down the street wearing a star: it meant that anyone could spit on us, or kick us as they liked. However, generally, they did not do that. What they did was worse than that: they showed a mixture of disgust and indifference as they bore our presence, hoping that we would be taken away soon. The young men were called up, Gyuri had to go, too. We said goodbye to each other, as if we were going to our separate deaths. I tried to convince him to commit suicide together, but luckily he was an optimist. He came back on the third day: he was sent to a hospital. How-

ever, he got bad papers: they said he was healthy. We said goodbye again, but on the third day he came back again: he got two weeks off before he was examined again. Two weeks later, we forged the date of his leave, which meant he could stay two more weeks. After that, I did not let him go back any more. We moved to the Kepes family in the meantime. It was Mom and Dad's second move, so they hardly had anything left. (One left behind more and more of the things we had thought indispensable before, so in the end we had one bag altogether.) On that day, Pest looked like a huge garbage heap. Half of the city's inhabitants had to move, and the other half watched this, gloating over the sight. In many Jewish houses, people just lived from day to day. Putting money away had no sense, they didn't buy anything for the long run, only food. People ate and drank like crazy. Many had earned a lot of money during the previous years, and they thought they would feed themselves well before being deported.

The tension eased a bit by the end of the summer: some people stopped wearing their stars. Gyuri changed his status from that of a deserter to the more secure position of a Paraguayan citizen, which was then extended to Mom and Dad and Ági Kepes as well. Gyuri could move freely now, so he joined the resistance, and worked for the International Red Cross, too. He managed to get many people out from different internment camps, and we got our apartment back, although we could not enjoy it for a very long time. On October 15, 1945, Ferenc Szálasi (Hungarian Fascist leader) came into power. My life was a nightmare from then on until the liberation. The Hungarian Nazi air raid officer told us immediately that we had to leave the apartment within the next 24 hours. Besides us (Mom, Dad and me) a number of army and forced labor service deserters lived there – Gyuri K. was also among the latter. So they also became homeless now. Gyuri went out to the convent to Klári. We went out to find a place that evening, and settled that Gyuri would come back the next morning for Mom and Dad. Unfortunately, the Nazi officer threw them out before Gyuri arrived, and he also forced them to sew back their stars. They were herded into an unknown Jewish house, from which Dad was taken away later, when they collected all the men. Gyuri managed to bring him back only two weeks later: just in time, as the unit was starting out to Western Hungary right then, that night. Only two people returned from that unit.

Mom and János (*my mother's brother, an adolescent at that time*) went to a camp protected by the International Red Cross, and Dad joined them there. Later Lili, Marika and Imre H. got in there, too. Gyuri and I lived at random places. Practically every day we slept somewhere else. By that time I was working for the Red Cross too, without papers, trusting that a miracle would happen. I was lucky. Once I arrived right after a roundup, and the next time I left two minutes before one. Gyuri recruited a few Hungarian gendarmes into the resistance movement, and they provided him with a detective ID, so he could go anywhere happily. He went out to the brick factory every day (that's where the Jews were deported from), and brought people, especially children back. There were small children every day, dozens of them, we didn't even know their names: their parents or acquaintances left them there in the tenement hall. In December the Hungarian Nazis (Nyilasok) suddenly invaded the camp in which Mom and the others lived: they killed the leaders, and herded the others into railway cars. Gyuri managed to arrange in the end that those who had not been taken away yet were brought back to the ghetto. Mom and the others got there, and then we brought them out into a Red Cross hospital, which was protected by the Nazis in that district who wanted to score some good points, saying that "one can never know how it will all end". They stayed there till the end. The hospital was hit several times, but they were not hurt at all, thank G-d. By Christmas, it was completely crazy. The Nazis killed anyone they found. People in the resistance also managed to kill a few Nazis, but that was only a drop in the bucket. The Russian assault is among my worst memories. I hadn't been so much afraid of the Nazis – but now I was convinced that I would not survive the assault. I was almost right. A bomb hit the cellar of that house, and everyone died who was in there: we were lucky, as we didn't manage to get in, it was too full, so we stayed in a basement room. We couldn't really enjoy the arrival of the Russians either, as the Germans took the place back on that day, and we were only liberated on the next morning. Then everything became wonderful. I still cannot believe that I am alive, and I feel as if this is a gift I have to earn from now on. I am thankful for the opportunity that I can see this dead, starving, ruined city resuscitate. I feel as if Pest was mine, and I have begun to like it – just as much as I used to hate it before.

The first things we could buy after the fighting was over were calendars and combs – out on the street, of course. Then people began to sell cakes, mostly made of corn flour. Then the whole *Nagykörút* became full of vendors, it looked just like a huge fair, but it was even more crowded. We met people we knew whenever we went there. In the beginning, we would be very happy. Later, slowly, it dawned on us that people were missing. And it's only now that we feel the pain; now that things are getting back to normal and it doesn't take all one's energy just to survive.

We became harder, and I have learned that one must actively take part in shaping one's own future: I will never be so helpless again. I won't just let myself be put here and there, not knowing what to do, and if (God save us) something similarly terrible happens in my life, well, then it was useful. My daughter, Anna Mária is a 'grown-up' five week old woman: I hope that by the time she grows up, she will be rolling with laughter when we tell her that once there were air raids, and then everyone rushed down to a cellar when they heard a signal, to sit there for hours, and then rushed back up, just to do the whole thing again 30 minutes later. Gyuri works in the Party, I am going to university (I'm going to be a doctor, I used to be a scrub nurse), and Anna Mária is growing.

I wish you all the best, too, and I am sending my kisses,

Zsuzsa

(*I don't know what would have happened if my mother had been told about everything that was to come, if someone had revealed the future to her, drawing aside the curtain just for a moment. Many things happened to her, to them. I don't know how she would have summed it up in the end.*)

Translation by Bea Sándor

Anna Aczél
Anna Aczél lives in Budapest with her family.
She is the director of a girl's home. She is involved in the rehabilitation of young deviant people.

Mária Herczog

THE TWO ANNAS

This story is dedicated to my mother's memory.
I wrote it in memory of her and about her. She did not live to see that I have become mature and accepting enough to tell her that now I understand and can appreciate many things I resisted and used to be angry about when I was a child, and even later.

It is a small consolation for both the child and the mother that someone was unable to become the kind of mother a child needs, i.e. an emotionally supportive person, because of the circumstances and the injuries caused by history, because of unprocessed traumas, or traumas that cannot be processed at all. It is partly for this reason, or in spite of it, that we must tell our stories, which might help other people to understand theirs and the difficulties others have.

My mother did not want to talk about the concentration camp, neither to me, nor to others. My grandmother, however, used to tell me stories about those times, in the room we shared, at night, after the lights were switched off. She talked about moving into a house marked by a yellow Star of David; how they lost everything; how my mother was taken away; about the siege; and about the time the Russians liberated them, how they didn't get back any of their possessions which they'd left for safekeeping, nor their apartment, and finally how my mother came back.

I had enough reasons to be anxious anyway, but these stories were extremely upsetting. It is no wonder that even 15 years after the war I kept playing "bunker" with my dolls: I spread the ironing blanket over the table in the dining-room, and hid under there with my dolls, equipping myself with lamps and food. Food, hiding and escaping played a central role in my games. My mother was truly flabbergasted once, when she was cleaning under my bed and found a small suitcase packed with underwear, a pullover she thought had been lost and canned food. These were the necessary preparations for being able to leave immediately in case the German and Hungarian Nazis came back. My mother, like so many other people thought that if she did not share her experiences with me, then, that part of her past did not exist any more, and the experiences were not "passed on". She always waved her hand, quite airily: it cannot happen any more, there's nothing to be afraid of, to play "bunker" is a silly thing to do. Because of this attitude, I have only sporadic information about her story and her demons, of which I learned much later. But the fundamental experience explains a lot about the reasons for her refusal to deal with these problems. After the establishment of the Hungarian Jewish Cultural Association, when *Teréz Virág* gave lectures about processing traumas and the difficulties of the 'second generation', I asked her to come with me, but she was reluctant. I still think that it might have helped, and who knows, maybe she might not have died at such a young age if she'd been able to unburden herself.

A few weeks after March 19, 1944, (the day the German Nazis occupied Hungary) two teenage *Annas* moved into the same house. Special circumstances played a role here: both families had to leave their original apartments, and had to move into a house marked by a yellow Star of David. They didn't have much time to think: they were given 24 hours to pack their belongings and leave their homes.

My 17 year old mother and my widowed grandmother moved into one of the houses on *Visegradi* Street where some of their relatives had already been living. One day in October, the people living there heard shouting from the ground floor: "all the women between 16 and 40 years of age, should come down, to be recruited for work." My mother knew what was awaiting her. They had information: she always thought that whoever did not close his or her ears knew what the facts were. However, most of the "adults" did not want to acknowledge that people were deported to concentration camps where they had barely any chance to survive. My grandmother packed only the most necessary things into a neat little cardboard suitcase, and made sure my mother left properly attired: wearing a suit and walking shoes that were fit for a young lady. She equipped her with a woolen blanket and food, as if she were going on a picnic. They had to walk a lot, and then they were deported by train to *Spandau*, a labor camp set up in a suburb of Berlin.

The Russians liberated this camp at the end of the war. My mother contracted typhoid fever. As a result of being sick she had to spend three months somewhere during her homebound journey. Nobody knew what had happened to her in the camp. We could only guess. She was not willing to talk about it. I only know scraps of stories: about too much work; humiliating treatment; abuses; being cold and hungry; and about frightening Alsatian dogs. She said that some of the girls there would talk about tea parties in their former homes, and would pretend to eat the those tea time delicacies. She said that the young women from similar backgrounds to hers showed very little solidarity which deeply disappointed her. But that she really appreciated the way the Soviet partisan girls, prostitutes and Roma women behaved. This shaped her world view and her affiliations later in life. She got home in August 1945, bald, weighing 35 kilograms. She went to visit her relatives as she didn't find my grandmother at home and they did not recognize her.

My mother's later life was shadowed not only by the war and the concentration camp experience but also by my grandmother's behavior. She felt unloved by her.

My mother never managed to have what she wanted in life. In spite of her intelligence, education and sensitivity, she never realized her ambition of becoming a stage director and dramaturge. The *Ratkó*-era turned her into a mother and that didn't make life easier for any of us. My father left the country in 1956. This created additional hardships and our subsequent years were no picnic.

On that same fateful October day, when one Anna was deported, the other Anna, who was exactly my mother's age, was living on the second floor of the same building with her parents. They were relatives of the owner of the house, so they moved into the family's apartment. Anna was hidden in the apartment, and her family would not let her leave when the Hungarian Nazis came to round everyone up. They hoped that the Nazis would not discover Anna in hiding.

At the time of the liberation she was still hiding in the apartment. During the bombing Anna didn't dare go down into the cellar, lest the concierge of the building should see her and report her to the police.

The liberating Russian soldiers found her while she was on the lookout for German Nazis and Arrow Cross fascists. As fate would have it, some of the Russian soldiers raped her, several times. She contracted syphilis, never wanted to have children and became a bitter, joyless, tough woman whose marriages never worked out either. I spent a lot of time with them when I was a child, without knowing her harrowing story. Nobody ever mentioned what happened. I know about this episode in Anna's life from other people.

There isn't really a good answer to all this. No one knows what should have been done and what should have been avoided in those days – what would help or what causes even more trouble. People did what they could, under those uncertain circumstances and what they thought was the right thing to do, at the time.

It is pointless now to pass judgment and we are definitely not the ones to do so. But we should discuss more the ideas that could give us solace; or, how to heal the wounds; and about how we can possibly let go of these terrible experiences that have become our heritage.

Translation by Bea Sándor

Mária Herczog

Dr. Mária Herczog was born in Budapest in 1954. She has a PhD in Sociology.

She works as head of the Institute of Criminology and of the Institute of National Family and Social Policy. Her area of research is the welfare and protection of children. She teaches part time at the ELTE. Since 1993 she has been Editor-in-Chief of the bi-monthly journal called Family, Child, Youth-published by the institute of the same name. In this institute she engages in research, organizes conferences and also works as a mediator and consultant.

Klári László

AT MY GRANDMOTHER'S FEET

I grew up as a child of the Holocaust. I was pretty well at home in the camps, wondered in and out. I was familiar with places, names, faces and dishes. No! There were no dishes; instead there were curious sounding stuff, such as *dörgemüse.* And hunger!

I knew the *lagerführers,* the SS female guards, and the *kapos.* I learned strange words like *appelplatz, heftling,* and *blockelteste.* I could see those barracks from inside out. I walked in the *forced marches.* I was there at the *selections.* All those belonging to me were always sent to the right. We were fortunate!

A typical scene from my childhood: My grandmother is telling me stories while I sit at her feet on a small stool. Her stories began early. Perhaps I was five years old when my grandma started.

"At night they banged on our windows," she tells me, and together with her two adult daughters she started to walk toward the "Kossuth Lajos" School. This school was the designated *ghetto* for the Jews of Esztergom and vicinity. Reportedly, grandma threw all her gold into the school's toilet and flushed it down. Was she aware of something?

A while later, during the early hours of dawn, not to be noticed by anyone, all of them were taken to the railway station, and forced into the cars. "Cattle cars", said my grandmother and I could actually hear the loud rattle of the cattle cars' heavy doors closing in on them. I could see the childlike *gendarmerie,* which my grandmother asked "My son, why do you do this to us, we are Hungarians too".

The train first went to Komárom and then for many days, nobody knew to where they were heading?

At this point, my mother would interrupt, if she were within earshot. Indeed, we had no idea where we were going but we were terribly crowded.

I was squeezed into a corner, and my shoulder was damaged and it is still painful. When my mother left the room, my grandma turned towards me and said. You heard what she said? She wasn't even standing there but I do believe that her shoulders still hurt because she was holding up, with her shoulders, for hours, your father's dead mother, your grandmother Fáni Sulc. But she wasn't my grandmother; I would insist at this point, she was my father's mother. I just can't call her 'grandmother'. "If you don't want, you don't have to. Also, there was in the cattle car your father's first wife too..." here she stopped. If, inadvertently, my father would walk in, my grandmother would stop talking immediately and would whisper to my mother "pszt don't, Zoli is here". They wrapped my father into the silence of forgetting.

Finally, we arrived somewhere. The tracks ended. This was the last stop. A weird place. On one side pyres are burning. One gate, one ramp.

This is the point where my mother would interrupt the second time: "I went first," she used to say, and behind me were Julika and then mother. When we arrived to the front of the line, a good looking, tall man, dressed in impeccable military uniform, was indicating with his forefinger only: to left, to right, to left, to right."

I was sent to the right and suddenly I froze. I lost track of time, space and place. I just walked on. I am not sure what distance. It happened in thousands of a second. Slowly, I turned around and I saw Julika behind me and above her head I saw mother's head. I breathed easier. Now nothing grave can happen," she would say.

I sit on the small stool. Grandma is unusually quiet. Suddenly, I am all confused by the right and by the left. I am left-handed, then what, which way? And what is on the left side? Who are there and what's with them? What about the fire? The noise? The odour? The smoke? – I heard a lot about them. But I don't ask. I had more than enough.

"In the early dawn, we are standing on the *appelplatz* in the nude, heads shaven. The sun didn't rise yet. We are shivering. No hair, which would warm us." I hear my grandma's voice. *I see the appelplatz. Right, across from me is grandma's face, because this time I am not sitting on my small stool. I am in my bed shivering. I am sick. The sun rose. It is very warm. Terribly hot. The sun burns me. I am feverish. There are those who couldn't stand any longer. They collapse. They disappear. If the counting is accurate we may leave. Bodies are left on the ground. I fall asleep.*

"Three weeks have passed". This is how grandma begins the next phase. "By then, your Aunt Julika is almost at the end of her sanity. For supper they usually gave us kvargli but after, no water or any kind of liquid. On all water faucets in the camp there are signs 'contaminated water, forbidden to drink'. Your Aunt Julika literally went crazy. She was screaming: thirst is worse than hunger and was running towards a dirty puddle of water. I caught her and held her tightly. That calmed her down a bit. Fortunately, that day we went to the showers. From the showerheads, alternately, flowed warm and cold water. Julika didn't care which one, she tossed her head back, opened her mouth and didn't just drink the flowing water but greedily tried to hoard as much into her mouth as she could. Her tears of joy flowing, mingling with the water to comfort her tortured insides."

"A few days later a rash appeared on her body. Not everywhere. Mainly on the arms and legs. Her legs looked particularly awful, full of reddish, pustules. I exchanged my bread ration for paper, and with my saliva-soaked paper I covered the spots" – grandma used tell this with the most vivid descriptions.

Yesterday, while I visited my son, he cut his hand with an old saw. He looked at me with desperation and asked, "Will this cause me blood poising? I told him to soak a paper napkin with his saliva and cover the wound tightly with it. On the way home, I reflected how I continued with the story about the sores. Grandma used to tell this so frequently that it stayed within me in its entirety. I am imprisoned by its tragic meaning but I am embarrassed when I use it.

"One day some kind of delegation came into the camp" grandma would start or continue, depending if I was already in place at her feet, or just sat down on my little stool for a few minutes. This was my prerogative. I could flee from her stories forever but I didn't want to.

"The delegation," she went on, "consisted of several SS officers, few of them women. We all had to line up, not as usually, behind each other but beside each other, in one line. This was an ominous sign. This wasn't a delegation. This wasn't a *zehlappel.* This was *Selection!* Shortly, the inevitable truck also appeared. This vehicle was used to cart away those who were *selected out* "– used to explain my grandma.

I hated that word 'selection' and I feel the same way even today. Thousands of images, voices, screams and tears are interwoven with it and with its unbearable burden.

"In the meantime, a tall, skinny, SS woman, her hair tightly pulled into a bun under her cap, standing at a distance from us, started to stroll slowly in front of our line, looking mainly at our legs", flowed my grandma's story. At this point in the story, she usually lowered her voice and started to tremble.

This didn't last long. She usually repeated it by shouting "she looked at the legs!" When she stopped at Julika, with her chin, indicated toward the truck. It was a hardly perceptible signal considering that it could mean a death sentence. My grandmother, (here I used to feel embarrassed), ran out of the line, dropped to her knees in front of the woman and pleaded; "Meine tochter!" My daughter! The SS woman hinted ever so slightly and Julika stayed in the line.

"We have been marching for days towards East." *This is the part of her story during which I just stared at her being incapable of believing that the person she was talking about is actually she, herself. It had to be someone else.* "We were marching, five abreast"- "The three of us at one end, because your mother would walk only at the outer edge, due to her claustrophobia."

"Well, not only for that reason", my mother would interrupt, "rather, mainly because a few kilometers earlier, a girl in our line, asked me to change places with her. She said she was afraid to be lying at the very edge, she felt safer in an inside spot – at this point we were all laying flat on the ground because of an air raid. The planes were flying so low that I can see, even now, the pilots' faces and they shot the girl dead on the very spot where I lay just a few minutes earlier, the second space, counting from the edge. I decided then that I always want to be on the outer edge. I can't sit anywhere else in the cinema or theatre than in the number one seat, my mother stated."

I remembered, that as soon as she would buy her ticket she would say, please, seat number one. Now, I also recall that my own daughter, many,

many years later asked me, "Mommy, why do you ask always for the first seat in a row?" I couldn't possibly answer her because if I could I would have told her that 'I could still see the faces of the pilots', but that wouldn't have made any sense to her.

"As we were marching," grandma would continue, "I, in the middle, on one side of me Magda Kövesi and on the other Julika Kövesi. I was wearing a 'garment' cut from a sack, a walking stick in my hand and a belt on which hung my dish. As we were marching, a military jeep passes by. In it sits an SS woman with a gun in her hand. It was her job to shoot all those who were collapsing. Several shots were heard behind us too, one after another – then silence. It was too silent. I look at my left and where Magda Kövesi walked a minute ago, now, nobody. Oh, my God, what will I tell those who'll ask me at home where did you leave Magda Kövesi, why didn't you take better care of her? What will I say?"

I felt like a robot. I couldn't ever understand this sentence of grandma's until later when I saw in a film the returning, robot-like, walking skeletons with their angular movements and their unimaginable bodies.

Mrs. Istvan Kövesi went back to the end of the column where she spotted a hovel. She started to poke with her stick at all the bodies covered with straw until she found her ward, Magda Kövesi and dragged her back to the marchers, to lay down and rest because by then it was nightfall.

"By the morning, all those who remained in the barn were dead" – these were my grandma's closing words to this episode.

And I, sitting on the small stool, would start to tremble, with no mother and daughter and 'meine tochter', with someone beside me and now, she is nowhere, and what will I say if they ask, where did I leave her?

My mother has only one story. A painful, guilt-ridden, masochistic story that happened during the march as they were nearing the city of *Pilsen.*

By then, for days, they had hardly anything to eat. According to my grandmother, my Aunt, Julika ate grass, potato peels picked up on the road and later she was sucking on an empty toothpaste tube. However, the greater problem was not having any water to drink. "Suddenly, just as in a fairy tale," grandma would say, "from somewhere appeared a large horse-drawn wagon. It was loaded with beer caskets. The drivers, taken aback by the look of these pitiful, unsteady marchers, ever so carefully, started to drop caskets of beers on the ground. Unfortunately, some of the beer bottles fell out of the caskets and rolled all over the place. The women started to run for them while the guards were beating them wherever they could reach them."

At this junction my mother would interrupt because from here on it is her story. "Amidst the ruckus, the noise and the stampede I suddenly notice that one of the soldiers hit your grandmother so hard that the metal dish on her waist was flattened. At that very moment a bottle rolled to my feet.

It took only an instant in my brain to realize that if I run to my mother I'll loose the drink. As I was lifting the bottle in order to hide it in my trousers' long pocket, I see that others were attending to my unconscious mother...."

Even till this very day...the sentence is not finished and my mother is crying. And her story is always told in the present tense.

My grandmother never cried. My strength comes from her, but in reality, perhaps my mother's tears that sustained me.

Translation by Bea Sándor

Klári Kászló

Klári László was born in 1947 in Esztergom, Hungary. She considers herself as a "second generation" Holocaust survivor. From her mother's family, her grandmother, her mother and her Aunt survived. The fate of her father's family is wrapped in silence. Her present work is based on these two inheritances. She works with groups of survivors and rescuers. She has two children and two grandchildren.

Júlia Vajda

LEFT ON OUR OWN

For quite a while now, it occurred to me, time and again, what will become of us when *they* are all gone. What will become of us without *them*? We shall be left all alone. I remember *that* feeling from my childhood. Just like being the last child left in a kindergarten, whose parents have not yet arrived. Actually, this didn't happen to me. The worst that would happen that I wasn't among the first ones to be picked up by my parents. But, as fewer and fewer children would remain, I began to worry: what if they are not coming for me this time? It wasn't even that: it was an inexplicable feeling of uncertainty. A lump in the throat. A knot in the pit of the stomach. Nausea. It was getting stronger and stronger. I am going to throw up. I am not doing anything, just staring at the window. I can't see out, it's high up, and it is walled up with glass bricks. An utter uncertainty of existençe.

Yes, it is the same feeling. What is going to happen to us, to me, if they, who lived through the Shoah, will not be with us any more? I was anxious. At times, I woke up in the middle of the night, overwhelmed with this ominous feeling. Was it only a dream? I don't know. Perhaps it was. I broke out in a sweat. One cannot just outgrow this feeling. Yes, it is a childish feeling. Implying that we are *only children*. Only those who lived through *that* are adults. And when they cease to exist, we will all be children, at least those of us who understand this feeling. The others, for whom the Shoah doesn't matter, or at least not in this way, or who, God forbid, even deny it, will perhaps grow up – but they do not matter.

Then one day my friend, Éva Kovács called me (she knew about my anxiety), and told me that we were going to interview people who had been deported and survived. Both of us had been chosen for the crew of the Mauthausen Holocaust Archives.

We became the "Hungarian unit". The task of finding and interviewing Hungarian survivors had been assigned to us. It sounds absurd, but I was elated. Yes, however morbid it may sound, I was happy. After all, we can at least question them before they all leave us.

Of course, later I realized that I wasn't the only one who felt this way – *they* too were more than willing to talk about their experiences, for the simple reason that they will not take to the grave, their, as of yet, untold stories.

A few days after we undertook this "work", I met Ágnes Heller and asked her to help me find people who were „thus identified." Of course, there was an uneasy feeling about "the others, who did not seem to matter at this time", that we could not deal with those who had "only" been in Auschwitz or in Theresienstadt. But at least we found them. Ágnes was just preparing to hold a lecture in the old people's home, located on Páva Street. She called me the very next day, enthusiastically: she found two people.

I felt a surge of anxiety when I called Frigyes A. He asked me to postpone the interview, because his brother had died not long ago. He promised to call me later. The conversation with him left me exhausted, so I called Mrs. Sándor A. only the next day. She consented to an interview immediately, but she told me, while we were talking on the phone, that she had been interviewed also by the Shoah Foundation. This time, she agreed, yet to another interview, so that she could tell somebody about her experiences before she had to leave this world. But she stipulated one condition: that we could only meet once – because the previous interview upset her too much.

I visited her on a Sunday morning in the spring, in her small Tömő Street apartment. I was appalled by her living conditions. Her place was small, sparse – I could also say, miserable.

She was nice and offered me coffee. Then told me again that she had felt overwrought by the interview conducted by the Shoah Foundation and she wouldn't like me to come for a second time. And then we immediately started to record what she wanted to say. She was impatient. She wanted the whole thing to get over with and I was anxious. Partly, because I was afraid of what I was going to hear, and partly I worried about my interviewee – by this time I was calling her by her first name, Márta, at her request. This way, it was easier for her to talk and bear the recounting of her story in one sitting. On the other hand, I wondered, will I be able to ask everything I would like to according to the rules of my profession? To follow the dictate of those rules I have chosen for the questions I intended to ask, during this one time? Then, I felt ashamed thinking this way. What does it matter, anyway? Márta is the one who really matters.

Indeed, but it is also important that she should tell everything, for our sake and perhaps for herself, too. Yes, I was reassuring myself, telling our stories, talking about things is often a balm for a wounded person. But is it also true in this case? Can it still matter, be of use, even now, when sixty years have passed? How will I dare to ask questions? I teach my students to be courageous and ask everything: the interviewee will draw the line. She or he will indicate: this far and no further! This, of course is true but they are not survivors of the Shoah.

Hopefully, it must be better to talk about the horrors of the Shoah than carrying the burden silently, for decades. My grandmother, who was "only" – at least seeing from this perspective, "only" – in the Budapest ghetto, kept telling us her stories until she died. I was bored by them as a child, and also as a young adult. I felt, I knew them all by heart. So I didn't ask her anything. I never made further inquiries beyond what she told us. I regret that now. However, now I *must* ask Márta.

I must trust that if other traumas are alleviated by talking about them, it will also help her. The least I should worry about is that *I* will not be able to bear what I hear. Or, that I won't know what to do. After all I know, and I have experienced it many times as an interviewer and as a psychologist, that it is beneficial to cry. It is the best thing to do. It brings a sense of relief.

Márta is talking calmly, she is really collected. She talks about her life in chronological order, starting with memories of a happy childhood. A happy childhood that was soon overshadowed by anti-Semitism, which reached her village too – meaning a gradual exclusion from the friends of the family, the elite of the village. *"There was a wealthy Jewish family living in Jászjákóhalma, and they had a radio that could get broadcasts from all over the world. They had electricity, too, while we didn't. We only had a battery radio, and these people told us, despairingly, that the Jews are trans-*

ported to be taken to the gas chambers in Poland. And we said that it was nonsense, it could not be true. So, we were so... stupid, we were uninformed and childish."

Yesterday my young colleague, Máté, went to talk to an elderly survivor who told him it was not true that they had gone to the slaughterhouse like sheep. After all, nobody could imagine that something like this could or would ever happen.

It doesn't matter who is right but I am still preoccupied with it. As if I was replaying in my mind this film, again and again, hoping that at least once, it will end in a different way, and not with *that*. Perhaps, this once everything will take a turn for the better. I cannot stop reading those memoirs. Not only the ones written by Imre Kertész, Primo Levi or the other "major" writers. I read the ones that are poorly written, too – with the same expectation. Or, with the perverse desire to relive it again and again, everything that I didn't go through at *that* time. Because in my heart of hearts, I feel ashamed that I did not.

It doesn't count to be born afterwards. It simply means cheating. Because this question always emerges: what would *I* have done *there* and *then*? Of course, I have a more preferred position: as I am a Jew, this question is not difficult but it is there. It came up first when I was pregnant. I had to stand and wait in the hallway of my gynecologist for about an hour. I was holding Primo Levi's *The Drowned and the Saved* in my hands. It was strenuous to be standing there. And then this question occurred to me: how would I have endured THERE and THEN? This question has come back to me many times since then. Especially since I have been ill, and I can hardly walk even a hundred meters. Would they have shot me because I wouldn't have been able to keep the pace? Or, would I have been sent straight to be gassed? Or, would I have recovered, since we all know that certain ailments are pushed into the background in extreme situations?

Márta keeps on talking. Now come the more and more dreadful details. We are on the ramp in Auschwitz – she is separated from her father. Then her younger sister gets the scarlet fever, and she is separated from her and their mother. Marta too contracts the disease. She meets her younger sister in the barracks where people with scarlet fever are housed but they are separated from their mother. We already know that they were separated forever. They both recover from the disease. They are sent back to their old barracks. There's a selection. Her sister was sent to the left, she to the right – from Mengele's point of view. But opposite, from *their* own points of view. This is important. Because this way she doesn't have to go into talking about her sister's death. Instead, she can talk about the unbelievable representations of the Shoah. This helps. She has had pangs of conscience ever since, because she did not go with her. Although she remembers her sister beckoning, indicating to her to go with her.

But what kind of thing is this, beckoning her to go that way – to die? And this is not the end yet. The next story is coming.

A gas chamber from which she was pulled out. *"I wouldn't like to forget to mention that approximately 25 years ago, I know the date because I still had the black and white television set, there was a program on the TV in which they talked about the conviction of the murderers in Auschwitz, and the Obersturmbannführer who had dragged five of us out of the gas chamber, was shown in a close-up, and the news was that he was acquitted, without comment. And then everything went dark."* Even this is not enough. Here comes the baby who was murdered. The baby who was killed before it could have cried out and it was Márta who had to take the body out to the latrine. Just then, Mengele was coming towards her from the opposite direction but she managed to get away. Now, this is too much for me, too. Tears came to my eyes, I have to cry.

Márta is just talking, talking. The battlefront reaches Auschwitz, and the camp inmates are "moved"– to Mauthausen, and later to Lenzing, to a factory where she has to work.

"Let's have a rest!" We pause only for a few minutes – to go to the toilet, and then we continue. They were marching in rows of five towards the trains. A Swabian peasant boy who speaks Hungarian is nice to her at first, but then he beats her within an inch of her life with his gunstock. She says that if you mix with brutes, you become a brute.

Can I keep on listening to this? And how long can Márta keep on? She is so calm and composed. This discipline, which she forces upon herself, is what enables her to tell the whole story. But several hours have passed. Will there be time for me to ask questions? Will she last? We are resting again. It feels good, but I am afraid of having to finish before we get to the end. I offer that I'll come back another time. But no, she wouldn't like that. She would like to finish it today, as far as we can get to. I agree, although I can hardly bear it any more. This story with the newborn baby was too much for me. But how can I tell her that? Márta can endure; after all, she endured it all, then too.

She comes to the point of what happened after she got home, and the stories of the aftermath. That her uncle stole whatever small things had been left to her. The Anikó Szenes Home for Orphan Girls, where similar girls (I wanted to say small girls) lived. Well, they were small girls as for their age, but with all these behind them? If there is a forced growing up, then this is it. I am thinking of my mother. When I was a child, I didn't understand what the trouble was, or that there was a trouble, but I kept feeling anxious, like in the kindergarten. Now I know, I think I know, that my mother was anxious all the time throughout her short life of 53 years. Yes, she also had to grow up fast when she was ten. Of course, compared to Márta, she was lucky.

The ghetto in Budapest was not Auschwitz or Mauthausen. Her mother stayed alive. True, she adored her father. At least I think so. Of course, I never asked her to tell me her life story either. It's not only that I didn't tape-record it, but also I didn't even ask. It was always my grandmother who talked about the ghetto and I didn't ask anything. I didn't know that I should have, at that point. Today, I do ask. But now, of all my family, I can only ask my father. He replies that he doesn't have any memories of his childhood, only since the Germans came in. When the tanks appeared on Nádor Street.

But now it's Márta's turn. Is it perverse that I enjoy the horror stories? That I enjoy the opportunity of listening to them? That at least I make her tell me what I never could hear from my family? Perhaps it is. Of course, my grandmother's family, her younger sister and her parents had also departed through the chimneys in Auschwitz. Oh, I hate that I am protecting myself by also using these morbid expressions.

Finally, I have the chance to ask questions. Márta has finished her own story. She did it skillfully; she came back to the present. She is reprimanding Viktor Orbán and the neighbours, who avert their gaze every time they meet, ever since Orbán and his gang inciting people. This is hell – that she has to experience this at the age of eighty, and alone. She has no family, neither husband nor children, no other relatives. All her friends have passed away... What's left is the 'daycare center' for the elderly on Páva Street. Her sight is also failing, she can hardly see. I am unable to say anything when she remarks, „it has been enough." Although, I'd like her to live forever. It's not very nice of me but I would like that not so much for her sake but mainly for mine, even though I understand that she has really had enough.

I take photos of the few pictures she has and of her, too. That, she doesn't want, saying she has become rather ugly. I am glad that I managed to persuade her. No, for me she is not at all ugly. The way she holds herself up, after all she went through, she is beautiful.

I say goodbye. I am worried though, for I don't know what state she is in. She sees me out. I don't know whether we shall ever meet again, because she said she wouldn't like to continue the interview. We almost worked ourselves into the ground, really, both of us. She promised to copy a map for me, a map that shows where Lenzing is, which was a sub-camp of Mauthausen, where she had to work in a factory and she would call me.

That's good. I will have a chance to see that she has managed to survive this interview too. Perhaps she is only exhausted, just like I am.

On my way home, I am staggering in the street. Details of Márta's story are whirling through my brain. As if I craved for to be where she was – to experience the horror of horrors. I also feel like I am a weakling, and totally useless. But I also feel bad because of my whining about it all – this must be the real "Jewish nurse" role.

I get home. My children are waiting for me. My daughter is 11, my son is 17. I tell them what I heard. But not the newborn baby. I feel that my daughter shouldn't hear that. Even though I always dare to tell them everything. I do believe that the biggest burden is silence. But not this, not this time. The rest is too much, although they want me to tell them everything. As if this feeling, the feeling of 'we-have-to-listen-to-these-stories' was in them, at least in my daughter, too.

I keep telling everyone what I heard, for days, for weeks. Perhaps, until I'll do the next interview. From then on, I will tell both stories.

In the meantime, Márta obtained the copy of the map, so I go and visit her in the Páva Street Center for the elderly. She is happy to see me, takes me around, and shows where they held the Seder not long ago, even though they didn't observe it when she was a child. But now this is the only community she belongs to. This visit reassures me. Márta is fine. And she is happy to see me again. This means that it was good for her to tell me about all those experiences of hers.

Weeks pass by; we are working on other interviews. I am immersed in them. My phone rings suddenly – it is Márta. She calls only to thank me for the interview. Because this was the first time she felt relieved *since then*. Because my "*system*" was very good. That I let her talk. And I only asked questions about the things I didn't understand. She was always disturbed, disrupted by the questions the Shoah-interviewers asked. Even though they were nice. And she says she hopes I would go on working with this "*system.*"

I was ecstatic. Márta was definitely relieved after telling me her story – I can hardly believe she said that. It meant a lot to me both personally and as a professional. I feel vindicated when I say that this interviewing technique works very well.

Almost two years have passed since then: we talk from time to time, I visit her. Her sight is failing; she can hardly see anything now. She walks with a white stick. She called me the other day – when I had already started to write this text. She told me that she went to the Páva Street Museum to deposit "the stuff" – ours and the other one, which had been made by the Shoah Foundation. Because she doesn't know what the future brings and she had enough, anyway. This way, her neighbours will not be able to laugh at her.

My heart sinks. We begin to talk about this, that the "young lady" in the Páva Street Museum asked her: why would they laugh at her? How come, even someone from Budapest, someone who survived the ghetto, cannot understand her, so what could she expect from "a little youngster" like this one, however well intentioned she was. That she spent her whole life this way, not being understood. I am trying to understand her – while I know that it is almost impossible. I don't want to say clever things; I am not trying to calm her down, while I may not agree that her neighbours would laugh at her. But I leave that to her. I am also a bit afraid when I tell her that I have been writing about the third generation, that they also have their problems. She doesn't really hear it. And perhaps it is better that way. She doesn't need to know that.

Not only because it is obvious that suffering in the *camps* cannot be compared to anything. Not just because she was sterilized and as a result she couldn't find a companion, which remained 'never-to-be-mentioned' for her – but because she doesn't really have, and never had, anyone.

The liberation found her thrown upon a heap of dead bodies. She was so weak that she couldn't move. Then she was nourished and "saved" for the American liberators to come and try to rape her, and for her only surviving relative to take away what she had left – and still, all this does not matter compared to the fact that she has been living with these thoughts for sixty years; the feeling of guilt; that she murdered her sister because she did not go to the gas with her.

And of course, subconsciously, she is also angry with her sister, who was fifteen at *the time* and remained fifteen forever. Truly, after all this, it is really impossible to feel that life is beautiful.

Yes, I can enter this world of horrors, mediated by Márta, for a while, but even there I am surrounded by some kind of security. Since Márta is there with me, I can lean on her – and I also have a way out. I, unlike she, have also another world.

Epilogue

Márta died in May. She did not live to see this writing. But would she have been happy to see it? I am not sure. I don't know whether she would have consented to my mentioning her real name.

Her miserable, small apartment on the Tompa Street is empty now. The local government is putting ads in newspapers to look for her nonexistent inheritors. Her "wealth" that was left to her from her state compensation will revert to the state, as she did not leave a will. The Páva Street Day Centre for the elderly cannot inherit it – even though this could have saved it from its fate: the religious community liquidated it, because it wasn't profitable.

While Márta did buy her tombstone at the Kozma Street cemetery, she had taken her interviews to the Páva Street Museum two months before she died – "so that those neighbours would not laugh at her" – but she did not make out a will.

Translation by Ágnes Merényi

Júlia Vajda

Júlia Vajda is a child of survivors. She was born in Budapest. She studied math, sociology, psychology and psychoanalysis. She teaches at ELTE University, Faculty of Social Sciences, in the department of Sociology. She has two children.

Zsófia Bán

SEASHORE, DESERTED

Some sentences are etched into one's memory without immediately revealing their meaning. Though they fail to signify anything intelligible, they have a mysterious power that suggests they are significant nonetheless and therefore worth remembering. Naturally, remembering them is not a conscious affair. They record themselves, inescapably sticking to our memory's flypaper only to reappear later – who knows when and how – with their meaning suddenly crystallized and clear, as if by magic.

My mother was twenty years old in 1944 and, by the testimony of her photos, one of the most beautiful women I have ever seen. She kept some of this beauty even later when I would have a chance to witness it, though, compared to her former glory, these were only the random, scattered pieces of a pearl necklace. My grandfather was a veterinarian and the family immigrated to Hungary from Transylvania in the early '40s. They lived in Túrkeve for a while, and one of my favorite photos dates from this period: my mother and grandmother are coming down a street, holding a basket between them, apparently on the way to the market, as the basket is still empty. Well, my mother, wearing a just-going-to-the-market dress, is coming towards the camera (*whose* camera, I wonder?) down that dusty village street, like a diva modeling the latest summer collection on a Paris catwalk. I would admire her figure, graceful long limbs, and impeccable taste and elegance in the years to come. My admiration and pride were occasionally colored by a touch of sadness, due to the early realization that I would never be able to live up to her in any of this. I mostly take after my father, both in physical type and personality; what I unquestionably inherited from my mother, however, was a love of languages and a talent for learning them: she spoke seven languages herself. It is beyond ironic, then, that the person who gave me not only my mother tongue, but also my gift for all other languages, was someone that I could not communicate with in any language, not in any real sense of the word. Needless to say, we did talk to each other, or in each other's direction rather, but we didn't tell much. She didn't, because she couldn't, and I suppose I must have reflected this. Mother tongues I had plenty (two, since in Brazil, where I was born, I quickly learned Portuguese from my black Brazilian nanny), but the mother's language I was missing. From my point of view, my mother was essentially mute.

If I don't offer details of the story of their deportation to Theresienstadt, this is due to the serious limitations of my knowledge in this regard. The four of them—my mother, her sister and my grandparents—were all taken together from the countryside some time around the end of '44, I don't know exactly when. Then all four of them returned somehow.

My mother never said a single word about this, and her silence was so heavy that it never once occurred to me to try and break it. It wouldn't have worked. Whenever a topic like this came up, she fell silent; when war movies were shown on television, she would conspicuously leave the room; if something wasn't clear to me in what I read on the topic, I would never think of asking her for an explanation. And I did read a lot about this when I was in secondary school—it was something I couldn't easily get out of my head. My recurring nightmares are evidence of this: I would often dream of the Gestapo coming to our school, telling the Jews to stand up and taking them away. In a strange or even morbid way, I sort of wanted this to happen. I guess I wanted to claim a sense of community with those who actually had this happen to them. And, of course, it also had an aura of heroism, something quite attractive in the Hungary of the comatose seventies ("at least something would *happen*").

But my most abiding childhood memory about this is how we had to be considerate and spare my mothers' "nerves." If I were up to some mischief, my gentle father would scold me with "you know your mother must be spared these things." Why this was the case I never found out; there were only vague hints. And there were probably few things I hated more than having to apologize to her every single time when I "committed" something. As for my father, best known and loved for his legendary sense of humor and inexhaustible storehouse of anecdotes, well, he didn't tell any stories either—or at least not too many. Still, the little I do know I know from him. That he escaped from forced labor camp, for example, and got back home, following the Russian front. But I only found out much later that Uncle Dezső and his family – people we often visited as "relatives" – were actually relatives of my father's first wife and that she had died in Auschwitz. This was my father's turn to shroud himself in silence; it was only by detective work that I could at least find out what her name was. I made several futile attempts to learn a thing or two from my mother's sister, who emigrated to Israel, but she would always reply with the question: "Didn't *Vica* tell you about this?" No, Vica (the affectionate form of my mother's name used in her family) didn't tell me about this, or anything else ever. "What's the point in mulling over these ancient stories anyway?" grumbled my aunt, effectively closing the discussion.

Consequently, my sources were limited to the remaining documents, photos, and official cv's; all I could do was to pore over applications, forms, dates of birth and death, and letters, which only gave up a fragmented picture, if any picture at all. Instead of their untold stories, let me offer a little untold story of my own. You can hardly call it a story; it's more of a sign indicating a site of absence – a mark of the missing whole. Much like in Breughel's painting – *The Fall of Icarus* – that tiny little leg peeking out from below the sea.

My father was sent to Brazil in the fifties as a foreign trade official for the Hungarian state, and I was born there. My mother did not become pregnant until the fourth year of their marriage and the second of their stay in Brazil, and even then I suppose it was due to the beneficial effects of the local conditions and the distance from home. At this time my mother was 33 and my father 49. Even this one time giving birth was so hazardous for her health that her doctors advised her not to attempt another pregnancy. This is how I came to be an only child. My mother adored life in Brazil, loved the climate, the sea, the beauty of the fairytale city, the people, our affluence, and I suspect, last but not least, the distance that separated her from Europe.

Once she took me to the beach close to our apartment, a place we went to quite regularly. It might have been a weekend, because it was incredibly crowded, though the beaches of Rio are hardly deserted even on weekdays. She must have been distracted by something, because as I was wandering around I suddenly realized that I was completely lost: I couldn't see my mother anywhere. Being about six or seven at the time, I duly fell into desperation and started to walk along the beach, wailing loudly, so I could find her. I must have spent quite some time looking for her, assisted by well-meaning adults who tried to help me and asked me what my mother looked like and where I'd seen her last.

Suddenly I caught sight of her; she was standing with her back towards me. Speechless with happiness and relief, I approached her without a word. She was crying loudly and before she saw me I could hear her saying "God, even here, even here?!" I was unable to interpret these words and didn't even try that hard; instead, I happily fell into her arms. I was found, which was important, because this way the ocean could go on serving as a benevolent distancing power and not a new source of horror. And she was found, and this was important too, because if she was found, I was found, not lost any more. This is a strange talent mothers have, whether they speak or not. And when they are not found any more, what remains is the empty seashore.

The meaning of this sentence did not become clear to me until many years later, when triggered by a thought I can no longer recall, like some rare fish cast ashore, it suddenly jumped into my memory. By that time she was gone. After the end of his second term of official appointment, my father decided we would move back home to Hungary. (Why he did so is another story, and I dare say a *complicated* one, but I'm afraid my knowledge is bound to prove similarly limited on this one too.) Before long my mother became a menacingly proficient collector of illnesses, moving to progressively more serious ones. She finally died of cancer, at the age of sixty-one, fifteen years after our return to Hungary.

Translation by Katalin Orbán

Zsófia Bán

Zsófia Bán is a literary historian and critique. She pursues studies in the field of visual art, analysis of the relationship between image and text and post-modern theories. Her essays, papers, and critical articles have regularly been published in Hungarian and International journals and reviews. She is a docent at the American Studies Faculty, at the Eötvös Lóránd University. So far, she has published three books: Desire and De-Scription and Images of Postmodernism in the Late Poetry of William Carlos Williams (Amsterdam, Rodopi, 1000), Amerikaner (Budapest, Magvető, 2000) and Esti Iskola, (Budapest, Kalligram, 2007)

Nicole Katz

CONVERGENCE

One Jew says, just for argument's sake, because God knows a Jew loves a good argument, "Being a woman and being a Jew are two different things."

"How so?" says the other Jew.

"One is a burden and the other is a curse."

"Oi, so true. But there is a time when the woman and the Jew becomes a Jewish woman."

"Oh," says the other one, "when is that, nu? Is it when she's cooking in the kitchen? Or praying at shul behind the mechitzeh? Or is it when she's at the mikveh?"

Stop! You gotta be kidding! Not in my family, not with my upbringing. My head was jammed full of liberalism and secularism; culture and travel. Still, I do have some sweet memories of women in the kitchen doing Jewish things. My mother with her bustling meticulousness cooking for the high holidays, smells from the old country, cremsli and csusztatott palacsinta. And making haroses and matzes cake at Pesach with my sisters, the three of us together. Usually though, we just noshed and cracked jokes, but always in the kitchen. We never really spoke about being Jewish, but later we'd speak about politics; Israel and the Israel haters. And as for being women, well I suppose we spoke about that sometimes, through our bodies, and what they were doing. But most of the time it was about outwitting each other, and because of our happy confidence in each other's presence, we could be pretty funny.

Cliches about Jewish women and Yiddische mammes simply did not apply to my mother. She was skinny and hated the idea of us being fat. The words, "That's a waste of calories", are seared into my mind forever. She never pinched our cheeks and told us we were adorable, she didn't kvetch and cling, and she definitely didn't think we were geniuses. She didn't lay on the guilt and tears, she just screamed! She could be pretty terrifying too and had an excellent forehand.

The other Jewish women in my family also defied the stereotype. When I went in search of the past, I went to Transylvania to find my mother's people. It turned out they were Christians, who'd once been Jews, who'd once been Christians. In a word, confused. Over there, the women were not just dominant in number, but in everything else too. They were big, they talked loud, smart and fast, and if you didn't like their cooking, you'd better ask for seconds. They weren't very Jewish, but they were very woman.

"Nu, so tell me, when is a woman who is Jewish a Jewish woman?"
"When she is standing under the chuppeh. For it is in her duty to find a Jewish husband, and continue the ancient line, that the Jew and the woman in her are truly united."

Never mind that this stern and inflexible command clashed horribly with that secular, liberal upbringing, this one was never negotiable. In this, as in so much else, my father set the tone. Gently, firmly, and always with a smile. It made it hard to say no to him. All our Jewishness came from the remains of his Orthodox upbringing. But it was more than his love and respect for tradition, and more than his unshakeable belief that having an identity was paramount. It was about Shoah. It was always there. Oblique, but inescapable. A cold, hard rod of steel rammed through our sunny Sydney lives. Six million didn't die so that we should just disappear. This scarcely articulated but omnipresent thought tested us in strange and disturbing ways, for as we went about our lives, busy, secular big city lives, knowing and loving other people, there was always a point at which these affections were stunted, tainted and limited.

We were taught not to hate, but how can you not hate? My father was usually too polite to swear, but the occasional "fucking Nazis, fucking animals" did slip out. Not so my mother, from who we all learnt to curse and blaspheme, in stereo, old school and new. Long before I ever came to

Hungary I could already swear with the best of the Pesti cabbies. "Everyone is welcome in our home", was the way we were brought up, but how long for, and in just what capacity? Now those were some other things we didn't talk about. I don't believe my mother would have had the stamina and belief to insist on a Jewish husband, not because of any liberal impulse, but her atheist, Communist education must have somehow stuck. Having grown up motherless, and for all intents and purposes fatherless, not much in the way of Jewish culture trickled down in the wilderness of her childhood. The first time she saw a chuppeh was on her way down the aisle.

How I loathed the narrowness of this Divine injunction, how I longed to distance myself from it. From the injunction and all the xenophobes who clung to it. I would escape its poisonous tentacles that pursued me in my most intimate moments, that made me fear and mistrust those I loved. I would become one with the great heaving mass of humanity, I would obliterate those suffocating ghetto walls for good. With every boy I brought home, I fought against it.

There was my first love, Pedro. Spanish, Catholic and very macho. He was too young to fret over, still, his parents warned him that Jews liked to marry their own kind. Lucio had the face of a Renaissance prince and the manners of a pimp. He tried to talk me out of my Jewishness by insisting I was a racist. And there was John, the dispassionate wasp, who found my ethnicity quaint, if a little too exotic, but it was all a matter of indifference to him. And then there was Ali, the Semite, who loved me and railed bitterly against all religion and those who would impose their authority. He dreamt of a better world where we would all be one, Semite brothers and sisters, living side-by-side, in peace, love and harmony. And wouldn't it be nice? Wouldn't it? To never wonder anxiously if he's Jewish, to not care if he's of the faith, a member of the tribe. He was persuasive and passionate, but he was the wrong kind of Semite.

When I went to Hungary to find my past, I also found Daniel, a country boy from Pécs. His eyes were heavy-lidded, melancholic and alive. He spoke English like my father. We fell in love. He took me by the hand and led me under the chuppeh. And in that moment, I became the Jewish woman I was always fated to be.

Nicole Katz

Nicole Katz was born and raised in Sydney, Australia. She works as a writer and translator. She currently lives in Budapest with her husband and son.

Katalin Katz

MY FIRST ADMIRER

My dad was a good doctor and a lousy businessman. When we first arrived to Israel he worked at the *Kupat Cholim* (the Israeli National Health Service), but he also took my *vatik* (one who's been living in Israel for a long time) uncle's advice to work only part-time and to have a private practice as well. So he did, and the patients duly came along. They were from the poor neighboring Yemenite Jewish community, as well as the penniless bochers from Jerusalem. Once he was even called out into the street by the police to certify the death of someone run over by a car. My father never accepted money from any of them.

In 1959 I was thirteen and we'd already been living in Israel for three years. One hot, summer afternoon, around two, I'd just gotten back from school when there was a knock on the door. A yeshiva *bocher* was standing in the doorway. He was around 16 or 17, and flushed from the steaming heat he was turning his greasy, tattered hat in his sweaty hands. He looked embarrassed. His shirt, which had once been white and was now a greyish-brown, peeked out from beneath his kaftan which he wore buttoned right up to his neck. His *payes* dangled down to his chest. He wanted to see my father. He had an earache.

"My parents aren't at home, but my father's consulting days are Tuesdays and Thursdays."

"When will he be back?" he asked, ignoring what I'd just told him.

"Late in the evening. They went to Netanya to visit relatives."

"That's okay, I'll wait for him," he said and stood there on the doorstep.

I didn't have the heart to send him away. And then my curiosity was tickled, I'd never in my life spoken to a *real,* Orthodox Jew. Back in Pest, before we came to Israel, I thought everyone was Orthodox here, and so when we docked in Haifa port I was shocked to see so many *normal* people.

The *bocher* sat down on the sofa and stared straight ahead. I tried to make conversation.

"Where are you from?"

"Jerusalem," he said, gazing intently at the carpet.

After a while I gave up and went to my room, but I watched him from there to see what he was doing. He didn't move an inch.

Around four I started feeling sorry for him, "Poor thing," I thought, "he could die of boredom!" So I snuck back into the living room and turned the radio on. It was the daily Torah reading program with commentary. I looked at the bocher, I was a bit worried, wondering what he would think about such a non-orthodox interpretation of the Bible. He was listening with apparent curiosity, then muttered something under his breath.

"*Meshuges, meshuges...*"

I was startled.

"Do you want me to switch it off?"

"No, no, we haven't got a radio! It's interesting."

So, not only are they not supposed to look at girls, they're not supposed to listen to the radio either. But I saw he was interested. Probably in both... Still, conversation didn't seem to work at all.

I went back to my room but kept spying on him. After a while I realized it wasn't only curiosity that was nagging me. I'd forgotten about lunch altogether! It suddenly occurred to me that he must be hungry too. I didn't risk chatting again and just went straight into the kitchen and made two huge sandwiches with sliced tomatoes. I took the food into the living room on a large tray.

"Don't worry, it's kosher, everything's kosher in our house." I put the plate in front of him. Finally he looked at me.

"And have you taken *maaser* of it?" he pointed at the tomato.

"Sure I have!" I scurried back to the kitchen shamefaced. I knew what maaser was, we'd learnt it at school. It was the law stating that one tenth of all fruit, vegetable and grain crops were to be given away to the poor or left in the field for the needy. I quickly grabbed the biggest, ripest, most beautiful tomato out of the fridge and threw it in the bin. Meanwhile I tried to make it up with God: *"Please, don't be angry with him, he didn't commit any sin, or if this is a sin, then I am to blame, but don't be angry with me either, please, I only meant well!"*

When I went back in, not a crumb was left on his plate. Both of us were satisfied.

My parents got home at eight and were astonished to hear that a patient had been waiting for more than six hours.

"Nothing serious," said my father when the bocher left, "he'll be all right in a day or two."

A week later, on Wednesday afternoon at two, there was a knock at the door. It was the bocher again.

"My father's at home now," I said by way of greeting.

Dad led him to his consulting room and a few minutes later saw him out.

"I can't see anything wrong with your ear now, I can't understand why it's still so painful, son. I'm sure it'll feel better soon."

The following week my Mum let him in. I heard her say Dad was at home, but he had no consulting hours that day.

"And your daughter?" he blurted out, "Is she at home?"

She called my father over and he examined the bocher's ear again. It was sound as a bell. I had escaped into the bathroom and peeping through the keyhole I watched my father walk him to the door, pat him kindly on the shoulder and say:

"Now there's really no need for you to come again, son. If you want to play truant, next time try thinking of something new. Good-bye!"

Katalin Katz

Katalin Katz was born in Budapest and brought up in an Orthodox family. In 1956 she made aliyah with her parents when she was ten years old. She graduated as a psychologist and social worker and has been teaching social work at the Hebrew University of Jerusalem for many years now. She specializes in research on the Roma Holocaust, in 2005 she published her book on the Roma Holocaust in Hungarian ("Suppressed Memories") with Pont Publishing House.

Anna Salat

ALIYAH

It was 1992, or 5756, but it seems as if only a few months have passed since then. It's all still so fresh in my memory, especially those first few weeks. My daughter Eszter and I left quickly, but our decision to make aliyah was based on long cherished dreams. At the time, Eszter was very religious. She rigorously introduced kosher food into our two-member family, and she also dressed the part, wearing long skirts past the knee, and covered elbows too. On the plane, Eszter, wishing to assert her independence sat apart from me. She was growing up and needed to be alone. Accordingly she arranged with Sochnut that when we arrived she would live separately in a religious kibbutz. I was offered the temporary solution of the immigrant absorption center, which I accepted. I was full of worries, I'd never been separated from her before, and she was full of the hope of youthful independence…

When we stepped out of Ben Gurion airport, we were greeted by the palm trees, the salty air and sunshine! Such euphoria! We were home! We were Israeli citizens now and the country needed us! The people were friendly and cheerful and joyful music spilled out of the bus that came to collect Eszter. She waved me happily goodbye. I waved to her with a lump in my throat. Having raised her on my own all her life, it was painful to part like that, even though I'd been preparing myself for this moment since her birth… A taxi came to pick me up as promised. Within minutes the driver whisked me over to the reception center and unloaded my dozen or so bags onto the sidewalk and whizzed away again before I could say another word. The entrance was still another hundred elusive meters away. I could barely lift two bags at once let alone twelve. I stared dumbstruck at my life's possessions as the city pulsed around me, as the car horns honked continuously, and the smell of the sea mixed with falafel floated in the air. Eventually it occurred to me to make use of my Hebrew, basic as it was. I called out to a well dressed older woman passing by.

" You can say it in Hungarian," she said to me, "I also came from there once upon a time."

Of course, she'd recognized my accent. She helped me with my bags, and finally I was in.

There were chickens were running around inside the building! And from the cooking smells alone you could tell there were immigrants from Greece and India and who knows where else.

I got my room. It turned out that I would be sharing. Well, really, I didn't expect this. My roommate was not at home. The two beds just fit into the room, there was a hot plate for cooking and a small shower in the entrance. The window overlooked an intersection, it was humid and hot, and the air was full of smoke and rumbling engines. I thought of my quiet old apartment in Buda, with its pretty view and clean air, of the modest but secure living I'd left behind. But I didn't miss any of it. Just being here meant everything to me, all of it in its entirety was happiness itself for me.

Soon after my Argentinean roommate arrived. She immediately offered me some practical advice: to buy my own dishwashing liquid and washing powder, and where, because she didn't like sharing hers. The boys, on the other hand, she didn't mind sharing them. She had 16 hairbrushes and 23 combs, I counted them, but I didn't get time for all the eyeliners and the lipsticks. Just then there was a knock on the door. My beautiful daughter was standing there. (She really is beautiful, and she's even starred in two films.) She was furious. "Mama," she cried, "in the kibbutz they sent me to they eat pork!" That would have been too much even for me!

Only a few hours had passed and our independent lives were over! I was happy, she wasn't. One thing was certain, our situations were intolerable. I didn't want to share either the boys or the room, and Eszter couldn't eat pork. We had to do something immediately. The Hungarian woman who'd helped me with my bags came to mind. She'd given me her number so I called her up. She didn't know where we could go but offered to drive us anywhere in her car. Through the National Association of Kibbutzim and a recommendation from an acquaintance we found another religious kibbutz. We hoped that things would be different there…

The kibbutz was what you could call moderately observant. Once there we began an introductory program called, *First home in the new homeland.* Rivkit, the person in charge of new immigrants, was a young woman in her 30s whose parents had come to Israel via Germany. To my dismay Rivkit was like a precision instrument. I'd been hoping for a sympathetic ear to tell my story to, but alas, no. I could ask questions, but if the answers weren't in the program booklet then she just turned the page. She raced through the house rules which she then had me sign. All this with my beginners Hebrew, which meant I didn't really understand a thing.

In time I learnt, among other things, that we were not to stay a day longer than was exactly stipulated, and that we were not allowed to receive any guests. Nevertheless I was very happy with the caravan we were allocated, a kind of mobile home without wheels. It was clean, it had two little rooms and a kitchen. It meant a little independence for my little family.

I thought about all those people from Hungary who warned me about the hardships of immigrant life in Israel, who tried to talk me out of coming. I pitied them now, the crickets were not chirping for them, and the beautiful fragrant flowers weren't blooming for them either. There were only a few people who'd encouraged me to make aliyah. Among them was a man named Gabor who worked at the immigration office in Netanya. I'd met him on a previous trip when I went there to get some information. He wore a crochet kippah and tzitzit. He encouraged me and said how nice it would be if more Hungarians came to live in Israel. When I went back to Budapest he called me often and strengthened my resolve to make aliyah. And just as we were settling into our little caravan on the kibbutz the phone rang, it was Gabor.

After exchanging friendly greetings, he asked whether he could drop a bag off at our place as he was just passing through the area and that this small favor would help him enormously. It was the most natural thing in the world for me to say yes. He arrived within half an hour. He started to unload his car, carting all of his life belongings into our caravan! By the time I realized what was happening I had to resort to drastic measures so I locked the caravan door. And then Gabor started screaming at the top of his lungs that some people just came to Israel and got themselves all set up nicely without having to do a thing whereas he'd been alone and struggling for years. I started to get scared, he was clearly out of his mind.

I thought of someone I'd met earlier in the day on the kibbutz, a thoughtful, older woman, I hoped she'd know what to do. She did. She immediately had two muscular security guards sent over who got rid of Gabor and all his bags. I was hoping to avoid a scandal, I sensed the kibbutz authorities would not like my story, but alas, a scandal was unavoidable. The next day I was taken to the police station for questioning. It turns out that my friend Gabor was a drug addict. And it didn't matter what I said, it seemed that my kibbutz days were numbered.

I suppose I could have felt cheated, that Sochnut had promised something else, that all those stories I'd been told about what a warm, welcoming nest Israel would be were not entirely true. I suppose I could also say that the Zionist Association's manifesto was misleading. And maybe if I'd stayed in Hungary after 1989 I too might have profited from the regime change and become a rich entrepreneur and visited Israel and stayed at the King David. But then I would never know how good it felt to take home fresh fruit from the market that had been left there especially for me by the vendors. At that time in Israel it was customary to leave some produce out at the end of market for the new immigrants and the poor to take home. And what made that fruit taste all the sweeter was that, unlike in Hungary, there was no humiliation in taking it. I've never felt disappointed with my first experiences of life in Israel, only that if I'd never known them, my life would be that much poorer.

One last thing. In the kibbutz, as with most bad stories, there was also something good that happened. Someone at the kibbutz heard about the scandalous start to my new life in Israel. His curiosity was piqued. He came to meet me and that was the beginning of a long, deep and beautiful friendship. But that's another story altogether…

Translation by Anikó Bakonyi

Anna Salát

Anna Salát was born and still lives in Budapest. She works as a drama teacher. She is currently engaged in a project to create a Jewish theater with high school and university students.

Júlia Lángh

SOFT, GENTEEL ANTI-SEMITISM

The second wife of my mother's brother was a petite, delicate and perky little woman, with large brown eyes, dark hair and skin. She was always in for a laugh. I was born blond and blue-eyed but very soon became secretly convinced that this was some kind of a mistake. In my true self I had a dark complexion, a deep voice and black hair. (The deep voice was easy, I managed that within a few decades with a packet or two of cigarettes a day.) My aunt's colouring seemed to stand for something, for the way I wished to imagine myself from the earliest days of my adolescence, when the construction of one's identity is in full gear.

My uncle and aunt often took me on long walks to the hills, so I could leave behind the memories of my sick mother and of my father who had recently died. Once, on an early summer day when the sun was shining sweetly and there was a gentle breeze, my aunt unbuttoned her blouse as she walked. I just stared at her, it was simply not done. Then she took it off altogether and tied it around her waist and continued half naked across the sunlit field. "Lovely! Lovely!", she cried, like a prayer of thanksgiving, raising her arms up to heaven. The nipples on her small, pointed breasts grew very large and surprisingly dark, and their aureoles looked like goose flesh. I was so embarrassed, never having seen a woman's breast so exposed and what's more, a woman so enjoying freedom. I trotted along beside my aunt, envious. My god, how brave she is! How gorgeous it must be! But I dared not follow her, even though she encouraged me. "Come on, take it off!" In the end she stopped pushing, apparently aware of what I wasn't then, that I needed to be liberated by a man. All the same, I kept trying to liberate myself as best I could. To be different, to be as different from my family as possible!

My mother, when she tried to confine my behaviour to that which was expected of a genteel, middle class girl, always had her mother in mind. If

I chose to line my eyes with the black of a burnt match (no other make-up available), she moaned, "Don't do this to me", pressing her hand to her heart that was growing more and more sick, "You know your grandmother's going to tell me off about you. I don't want a row again!" I had my fair share of my grandmother's reproaches, too. "You look like someone on the job", she used to say. For a while I had no idea what "job" she was talking about. It took some time for me to get to know the word "whore" and identify it with the "job" grandmother so often mentioned. "What would your poor father say! Here we are, a family without a man and you behaving like that!"

Behavioural norms for grandmother were set by what people would say, which meant the neighbouring genteel society of Rozsa Domb. My mother's greatest concern was what her mother would say, consequently she tried to mould me with grandmother's values. I resented this. I wanted her to take me as I was, and what's more, to take my first love – a curly haired young poet in a canary-yellow corduroy jacket – as he was. And not to make intrusive remarks about why he'd stopped going to university. My grandmother's objection was much more sharply worded, "This Jewish boy has got no existence whatsoever." The fact that he was an unemployed poet without a job was just about as frightening for her as his being a Jew.

Later on, I announced at home that I was to get married. Not to the poet in the yellow jacket, but to my next love, with whom it was love at first sight, who proved to be the man of my life, with whom we later had two lovely children. Grandmother remarked, "What a fine, good-natured young man. Pity he's a Jew!" It soon turned out that my future mother-in-law had made a similar comment to her son about me, "Nice girl. Pity she's Christian." We had a good laugh about that, in private.

My grandmother was anti-Semitic in the way the Christian genteel upper crust generally were in the first half of the 20th century: involuntarily, unwittingly, and one might also say instinctively. However, during the war her honesty was also instinctive. In the air-raid shelter built for eighty there were two hundred of us were crammed together under the ruins of a five storey building. In this community of women, disabled old men and children she was singled out as boss of the shelter. My strong-minded grandmother kept strict but just discipline and her orders were never disobeyed. That's why she could hide some people, Jews and deserters, in a walled-in hiding place within the shelter. It never crossed anyone's mind to report her to the police, even if those in the shelter knew about her secret, which they probably didn't.

I was two years old when I got typhoid. My grandmother ran to the secret chamber in the shelter to find a doctor. Some of the bricks could be removed, which is how she handed food to them. "That Jewish doctor saved your life", she would tell me later, "and he had no medicine either, only good advice, 'Take the little girl out of this packed, unhealthy cellar, she should have some fresh air and then believe me she may even recover by herself.'" They believed him, so my mother walked with me in the heavily bombed city until she found a well-aired flat where we could stay.

My grandmother couldn't understand that after the war it was impossible to talk and think like before. Trembling and shuddering she mourned the unjust death of her mother-in-law, who was shot into the Danube. Still she went on with her little anti-Semitic remarks, just as any self-respecting genteel lady would. "Jew", in her vocabulary meant particular things, as did the word "Gypsy". It was she who involuntarily, of course, taught me to be proud of being "different". "You're not one of us", she'd say whenever she deemed it necessary to teach me a lesson. "Whenever I look at you I can't help thinking that the old family gossip might be true after all. Great-grandmother, out there alone on that remote Polish estate while her husband was away hunting in those dark, foggy woods, tiptoeing to the back gate of the castle to secretly let in the local Jew or a wandering Gypsy… and now their blood is taking their revenge. It shows on you clear as day!" And I, secretly, proudly raised my head at that thought.

"By the way", my grandmother would say – she often started her stories with "by the way" – "poor Béla had this acquaintance at the stock exchange, a very good man he was, a Jew, but they can be nice people of course, and he was an old hand at money!" Grandmother seldom brought up "poor Béla", her husband who died at a young age. She seemed to remember her brothers much more vividly. She was far from mournful when speaking about her dead, she was past missing them, yet she maintained an intimate relationship with them. One of her favourite stories was about her brother Józsi, who during the era of the Hungarian Soviet Republic – which she always referred to as "the Commune" – shouted to a friend across a crowded tram: "So what do you think about how these proles stink? Absolutely foul!" My grandmother truly appreciated this courageous act of opposing red terror. Her favourite brother, Géza, was a musician who for decades played the organ every Saturday in the Dohány Utca synagogue. Grandmother would tell me proudly, "Jews are very particular in their musical taste, they enjoy and understand music. Just think how good my poor darling must have been, to be the chief organist of the great synagogue of Budapest, and a goy!"

Sometimes she said things that made even my mother's hair stand on end. My mother was the embodiment of political correctness some fifty years before it was actually invented. "I fail to understand," my grandmother would mutter about the second marriage of her elder son, with an innocent smirk on her face, "why he keeps marrying Jewish girls when there are so many lovely Christian ones around..." True, she only mumbled it to herself and would never dare say it to her son. And she would never take a dig at her daughter-in-law's Jewishness. However she unfailingly picked on her other daughter-in-law for her "proletarian" background, not to her face, of course, but behind her back, certainly. Her younger son stuck out in the family for not having finished his schooling, and he had all kinds of odd jobs, from working in the sewers, in a butcher shop, to selling flowers, and eventually marrying a charwoman. To her lady friends my grandmother would say, "My little daughter-in-law works in a pharmacy." True, she worked in a pharmacy, as a charwoman.

Funnily enough everyone seemed to stick out of the family, at least by my grandmother's standards. Her oldest, favourite son – also my favourite uncle, whose second wife so fascinated me with her liberal ways on that outing – became a communist in the 30s out of moral outrage with the politics in that era. In the party he met his first wife Vera, a tall, heavily built Jewish girl with pronounced features who he married quite quickly, when "mixed marriages" were still allowed, and people believed they might even make a difference. Later they went into hiding together and when the were caught by the Arrow-Cross my uncle declared he was a Jew so that he wouldn't be separated from his wife. "He was made to strip off his trousers," my grandmother said enraged, "but it didn't matter that they saw he wasn't Jewish, he was taken down to the banks of the Danube just the same." At the time I didn't understand what she was talking about and I dared not ask.

Although it was hardly ever mentioned, this story left its mark on my childhood. I pieced it together like a puzzle from odd words and broken sentences:

My uncle, his wife and his mother-in-law are standing on the lower embankment of the icy Danube. The Arrow-Cross are shooting people into the river one by one. Vera's mother collapses into the icy water just as a military van pulls up. "These prisoners are ours!" yells someone from the van wearing a high-ranking German military uniform. Then he jumps out and brutally pushes those people who are still alive into the van. Among them my uncle and aunt, unwilling to break away from the icy water, in the hope of saving Vera's mother. Then a few blocks away he sets them all free with a single wave of hand. No one ever knew who he was and why he rescued them.

My uncle never spoke about his first wife who committed suicide shortly after the war. Nobody ever said a word about that in the family, but that scene on the embankment served as an explanation for me.

I don't quite remember when I first started having the dream, the nightmare, the recurring, sickening nightmare. For years it was with me:

There are many of us standing side by side in a line, waiting to be executed. I'm at the very end of the line. The firing squad is not in front of us and they're not behind us either, they're shooting at us from the side, from the far end of the line. As the bullets are flying at us sideways I may be able to survive as the others standing ahead of me in the long line are getting hit by all the bullets.

I don't know which is more agonizing: the terror of execution or the knowledge that I might escape while the others die from the bullets directed at me.

This nightmare, as well as another recurring nightmare, disappeared, never to return, as soon as I left Hungary in the 1970s.

Translation by Ágnes Merényi

Júlia Lángh

Júlia Lángh was born in 1942. She's worked as a teacher, in advertising, as a translator, a social worker and a journalist. From 1977 she lived and worked in Paris. In the mid-80s she worked for Radio Free Europe until its closure. In the mid-90s she lived and worked in Nigeria and Chad. In Nigeria she lived in the bush and worked mostly as a kindergarten teacher. In Chad she taught radio broadcasting to the physically challenged. She currently lives in Budapest and works as a translator and writer, publishing regularly in journals. She has also published three books: "Near Africa" (1996), "Back from Africa" (2002) and "A Genteel Girl from Buda" (2003).

Anna Valachi

CONFESSION OF A "SPIRITUALLY" JEWISH WOMAN

I was fifteen when I learned that my classmates thought I was Jewish. Back then I hadn't yet heard about the Székely Sabbatarians who'd been so enchanted by the world of the Old Testament that they'd converted to Judaism of their own free will, observed the religious rules of the book of Moses and also shared the tragic fate of Jews born during the Holocaust.

A few years ago when I read Géza Szávai's book *Székely Jerusalem* about the tribulations of these "spiritual Jews", the Transylvanian Sabbatarians, I rejoiced with the realization that this new "category of identity" fitted me precisely. But only recently have I started to look for answers to the increasingly pressing question: why do I find it appealing to be considered "different" in our world which is so prone to discrimination? The explanation was to be found – like to so many vital problems and dilemmas – in my childhood experiences, recalled from a dim and distant past.

I've never belonged to the safe warm masses of any majority. As a result of my deeply religious aunt's christening in the Hungarian Reformed Church, my parents decided to raise me as an atheist. When I was nine, my father got promoted, he became very prominent in our local community and in the Communist Party. From then on I shared the fate of other stigmatised individuals. I only had to introduce myself and everyone knew where came from. My family name almost felt like a "yellow star", to be constantly worn and stared at by others.

My "privileged" social status hindered rather than helped me establish relationships and achieve self-realisation. I could never be certain why adults or even my contemporaries were friendly with me; they may have been instructed by their parents to be practical in their social behaviour: "being friendly with a cadre's daughter might prove very useful".

I sensed the hypocrisy though and ran away from fake friendships. Everyone was afraid of my father because he seemed like a very stern, even severe person – although he was always ready for a good laugh in the family or with friends. But I was the only one to know this – his colleagues, my teachers, my classmates and their parents only saw the powerful man.

As I was growing up, I longed more and more to be distant from my family but had no one to share my dreams with. Ever since I was first taken to the theatre at the age of five I wanted to become an actress more than anything else because an actress can live as many lives as roles she plays. At primary school I was regarded as the best reciter of poems in our district, so I refused to see my future in any other profession. In the sixth grade, that is at the age of twelve, after changing schools, I finally found my "true", trusted friend to whom I could honestly open up my soul. She also needed me. Zsuzsi's family was Jewish and our classmates, while they liked her, considered her "different". Uncle J., my friend's father was a relatively well-to-do craftsman, still, they lived very modestly in a flat of two rooms and a kitchen in an old, one-storey house with a porch. True, they were the only ones in the neighbourhood who had a television in the early sixties but they welcomed everyone who knocked at their door. On broadcasting days the neighbours flooded their flat.

Zsuzsi – born on December 13, on St. Lucia's day – was in fact only six months older than I was but as far as experience and wisdom were considered she was a thousand years older. She carefully tried to hide that from the world, though. She wore her long black hair in pigtails down to her waist; she was a sickly, pale child with a soft complexion and a fragile, lean body. But she had an open, eager and emphatic mind and was just as friendly as her parents. Father J. – that is Uncle Náci, pronounced Nazi, (his original name being Ignác but all the family called him by this nickname since he was a child in spite of the terrible associations), welcomed me with a broad smile and loud cheers whenever I met him. But he was seldom at home. His wife, a small, plump, active, merry and hearty lady kept house. My impression was that Auntie J. was worried about her teenage daughter but apparently also respected her, whereas she mollycoddled her son, the nine year old, red-haired, freckled Tomi.

I loved to stay at their place because there I had the feeling I was in a real home, much more than with my own family. My parents worked in important positions from morning till night and both came home angry, irritated and exhausted. I had no idea and was not interested in what gave them a headache. Neither was I interested in what was going on at the turn of the fifties and sixties in politics. I was preoccupied with my own emotional turmoil. What upset me most were my father's demands. Basically, I was proud of him but his strict expectations weighed on me heavily – he wanted my sister and I to be model pupils with excellent behaviour, problem-free daughters, held up as examples by our teachers. I suffered from these restrictions and duties, from the expectations of the outside world, but above all from the lack of parental love and understanding, and their lack of curiosity about my needs and wants. My beloved grandmother who always found and comforted me when I "ran away" in my unhappiness was very sick by then, therefore I couldn't count on her care.

Zsuzsi took her role.

I used to visit my friend mostly in the afternoons when I found her surrounded by books. She never let me feel I was disturbing her. As she glanced at me with curiously sparkling brown eyes and gave me an encouraging smile, I felt a sudden urge to talk. Otherwise, I was shy to talk about myself with others. I confided only to her that I was in love with a boy from the neighbourhood. He was Tamás, who recited poems beautifully. I heard him first to recite Attila József's poem *Ode*, and after he'd recited it in the courtyard – according to the instructions of Tibor Bodor, the actor – he also enthusiastically explained how to interpret the spiritualised and corporeal metaphors of that strange love poem. I sensed that it was troubling Tamás that I came from a different "background" and this made me almost angry with my parents. I could hardly wait to be a grown-up and rid of the "father-daughter" stigma.

Zsuzsi's dimly lit room lingers in my memory like the intimate space of a psychoanalytic consultation room. Sitting across from her it was like a therapist conducting reciprocal analysis with her patient. Though my friend spoke about herself less than I did, she let me know she wanted to be a writer. This took me by surprise, as it had never occurred to me before that it was possible to choose such a profession. Then I learned of the inspiration for the unusual career choice: it was *Anna Frank's Diary*. All the same we talked rather rarely about being Jewish and Jewish religious customs.

Once I knocked on their door at an inopportune time. This time, the, always cheerful, Auntie J. had a frightened smile on her face and opened the door in terrible embarrassment and closed it right away behind her back. She asked me to come back the day after as they had guests and had no time just then. Meanwhile strange, droning sounds came filtering through the kitchen, and on glancing in I caught sight of an old man with a long beard in a hat, swaying rapidly. He seemed to be familiar with their place and apparently he was celebrating some mysterious ceremony.

When I told my parents what I had seen at Zsuzsi's house my father informed me ceremoniously: "My dear, what you've seen was probably a Jewish religious service. Don't talk about that to anyone!"

(When I was a young child, starting kindergarten, he informed me, with the same stern face, that little Jesus does not exist and that I shouldn't believe the other silly children. Christmas is a religious holiday and only poor, narrow-minded, misguided people believe in God. Fortunately he never deprived me of my belief in Santa Claus – probably he considered him a politically neutral supernatural...)

When we met the next time I saw the same embarrassment on Zsuzsi's face as on her mother's the day before. With strangely blurred eyes and in a hushed voice my friend asked me not to tell my father what I saw at their house because that might get them into trouble. I was astonished to realize that this all encompassing "despicable fear" even got between the two of us. I didn't tell her, of course, that I'd already mentioned my strange experience at home and that my parents also made me promise to keep it secret. On the other hand, since my "initiation" I learned that it is not proper to visit religious Jews on a Friday night.

*

It was during our grammar school years when Uncle J. decided to emigrate to Israel with his family. Zsuzsi, who, by now, wore short cropped, modern hairdo which gave her a far more feminine look than when we first got to know each other, wanted desperately to stay but she couldn't possible object to her father's plan. She promised me to return as soon as she came of age. Till such time, we would correspond frequently and never get separated in our hearts. Parting was very sad for both of us. I felt broken without Zsuzsi, I avoided their neighbourhood for a time, even though Tamás lived there. Once, when I complained about my friend's absence to a classmate, she stared at me perplexed and said, "So why don't you people follow them there?"

It dawned on me then that our family was considered Jewish as well – probably because of my close friendship with Zsuzsi. I didn't object, it warmed my heart to have been identified with her. From then on it was easier for me to accept her absence: I carried her inside me as we shared the same roots, as far as the others were concerned.

In spite of her promise to come back, Zsuzsi never visited me, except once, twenty years later. We corresponded for a long time. She informed me that she was called up for military service, but it was beyond my imagination how such a delicate person could bear arms. All the same, her enthusiastic letters and especially a photo of herself in military uniform and seeing her radiantly happy, convinced me that she'd found her home in her new country. Eventually, she became a social worker not a writer, but her husband, who she met in the army, did some writing. They had twins, as a result of artificial insemination, because her husband was confined to a wheel-chair due to war injuries, but still Zsuzsi looked after him lovingly.

I learned several things about her life only afterwards and indirectly, because our correspondence stopped from the time of their visit in the early 80s. Ever since then, I've been listening to each newscast about the never-ending, bloody Palestinian-Israeli conflict, riots, wars and acts of terrorism, worrying about Zsuzsi and her people. The reason for her silence has also become clear by now. After forty years, fate brought me together with Tamás again, my childhood love and Zsuzsi's neighbour. From Tamas I gleaned that since the 80s an irrational fear had overcome Zsuzsi: she simply dared not write letters to Hungary for fear of causing harm to her friends living here. Her grown-up little brother, Tomi, is regularly in touch with Tamás, and I hope that sooner or later, with his intervention, we can get together again.

*

Looking back from a long-awaited future to my own past I believe that my "spiritual Jewishness" is a definite part of my life. Since my friend left I have become increasingly aware that owing to both my appearance and mentality many people still take me for "Zsuzsi", therefore I have a first hand experience of how the people I know relate to girls and women they regard as Jews. I have never argued with anyone, because I believe that a person is Jewish who is considered Jewish. When a colleague of mine confidentially asked my advice on what type of text book she should buy for her modern Hebrew language course, I apologized that I had no idea because I'd never learned that language.

As a woman, however, I was forced to "come out" from time to time: these moments are recorded in my memory as unpleasant, even depressing experiences.

When I was twenty-something, I fell in love with a nice, intelligent guy with a good sense of humour. Our relationship soon became serious, we were planning our future together when – at dinner in a restaurant – he mentioned that he insists on having a proper, religious Jewish wedding. – It's no problem – I shrugged my shoulder – I've no idea what it's really about. As a little girl we used to go to the Catholic Church each Saturday with my friends to admire weddings, but I, as a member of the Reformed Church, have never ever taken part in any wedding of a different religion.

He stared at me as if not hearing well. How come I never came up with that before? How could I let him believe that I was Jewish as well? How could I ever think he can introduce me to his parents? Tradition is tradition, after all! He's sorry it happened like this, he likes me a lot but marriage, unfortunately, is out of the question... Meanwhile the waiter brought us our dinner but I simply couldn't touch my food: instead, I was swallowing my tears all evening..

This form of rejection came as a shock to me: I decided from here on I would lay my cards on the table, from the start, never leaving people in doubt. Next time, the trouble was just that.

An acquaintance of mine, a few years older than me, was hanging around me for quite some time. He was doggedly courting me, so in the end we went out for a dinner. We started with cognac then had some wine with the dinner.. He may have gotten tipsy because at the end of the dinner he blurted out that although he was married, he fancied me and wanted to go out with me, because, as he admitted, he never had an affair with a Jewish woman and he heard that they are very sensuous and real masters in the art of love. I was dumbfounded. Zsuzsi and Auntie J. appeared before me, the first and most important "Jewish women" in my life whom I got to know closely. Sexuality was just about the last thing I would have associated them with. Today, I suspect that distorted literary descriptions may have inspired his imagination: he would have had ample opportunity to read about the voluptuousness and lascivious desires of the Jewish women of Pest in Dezső Szabó's infamous novel, *The Village Carried Away*, to mention just one such literary stereotype. I think it is astonishing, that this kind of literary fixation, flourishing at the turn of the last century, could still find an interested audience these days.

Right there and then, in an outrage, I told him the truth.

When he realized I meant every word I said, he pushed his plate aside grumpily. I'd spoiled his evening and shattered one of his illusions.

But sometimes there is justice in life, – as a partner to a "fake-Jewish" woman a similar husband was given. Scores of people think David is a Jew because of his first name, although it is an assumed name. Originally he was registered as József, after his father, but he sought a special first name for his common family name. What's more, he had a "real" Jewish wife before me, but the reason of their divorce was not because it was a "mixed" marriage. Among our friends we do not care about each other's origin, we make friends based exclusively on common interests and mutual sympathy.

I believe this to be proper.

Together with Géza Szávai, I believe in the survival of mankind on the highest level: "Connect to the fate of a stranger!" No two human beings are greater strangers to one another than a man and a woman who connect and through their children become kinsmen to the seventh generation and beyond. I believe that the ultimate condition of survival is the acceptance of that stranger, and of unconditional love.

Translation by Ágnes Merényi

Anna Valachi

Anna Valachi's main fields of research are the life and poetry of Attila József, the psychology of creation, and the relation of literature and psychoanalysis. She received her PhD in literature in 1999, and was awarded the Tibor Déry-prize that same year.

Zsuzsa Tamás

AM I A JEW?

To Gábor Németh

"The short film was black and white, and unlike the enthusiastic voice-over of the former film, this one had a serious and dispassionate voice, prosaic but stylish. They felt that they did not need to do much more: let the bare facts come, the images will do what they have to. They will fix things.

Me, for example.

I can hardly remember the words.

But I do remember the images.

A hundred thousand empty suitcases in some coop, stacks of hair, a million empty wire eyeglass frames, as if they had been made of coop wire, the glass carefully removed and the frames re-folded with something like angelic patience, so that nothing should be broken, long houses somewhere, a chimney smoking, photographs of men and women, impossibly skinny, to the point of death, and finally the bulldozers.

They pushed naked people into pits with those bulldozers.

Dead bodies, that is.

Naked dead bodies were waving there, a sea of bodies, as if someone had opened a wardrobe and the puppets had fallen out of it. It was the first time I saw dead bodies. Still, I didn't think they could have been asleep. I didn't think what was usual. How calm Grandma's face is, as if she had just fallen asleep. No. These did not seem calm. They did not seem to be grandmas. They did not seem to be anyone. There were too many of them to be someone. The someones were standing next to the pits wearing elegant clothes, probably uniforms, but I remember them wearing light summer suits and straw hats and pointing at the pit with their sticks. Bamboo walking sticks, not wands used for creating things.

I did not understand what the voice-over was saying, I don't remember the words, even though I once knew them all, now I don't remember a single word. Or I remember one word, only that one incomprehensible word. Probably because they used it to name the dead bodies. Or because I hadn't heard it before. And, as everyone knows, children are receptive to what is new. It was said as if it didn't just refer to the dead bodies, but also to the reason, the reason for this entire *process*.

The voice said they were Jews.

I understood that at least.

Jews. This means this is what had to be done with them.

Now I know that at least."

This was written by Gábor Németh, not me. Still, it is my computer that shows the message: "This sentence is too long, perhaps it should not be one sentence." And there is the word on my computer: Jew. And the image of the waving sea of dead bodies. It didn't hurt when I read it, but now that I put it aside, it does.

I am sitting in Bálint House, the Bálint Jewish Community Center, talking about Holocaust education, and someone remarks that it's not good if children only hear about the Jews in the context of the Holocaust. Why is she saying this? She says it would be important for the children to hear about it earlier. I am quoting myself. If Gábor Németh typed this for himself, he would see that this is perhaps not one sentence. So, the pedagogical point of view:

"A significant event of the 2000/2001 school year was that secondary schools from now on must observe Holocaust Memorial Day. This is, in theory, a huge step forward in the field of Holocaust education. But what does it mean in practice? (And does Holocaust education exist in Hungary at all?) The students are getting used to the fact that the Hungarian Holocaust Memorial Day is observed on April 16th; this is the fourth time they've held it. But what do students know about the Holocaust? Is it possible to learn anything essentially important about it during an obligatory memorial ceremony, standing in the gym, wearing a white shirt? Is it possible to commemorate the Holocaust in a crowd? And if it is not, what would be a worthy commemoration of this day in schools?

Several people have tried to answer this question. I myself have read applications about organizing a memorial day that was different from other commemorations, but I have also seen awful ideas, like the one about organizing a handicraft workshop where students would make yellow stars…

My own answer is that of a teacher of literature, someone who believes in the strength of words and literature. I would organize a confidential discussion about a book, between the class and a teacher." (Zsuzsa Tamás: *From awful things to faithlessness, or what shall we say about the Holocaust during literature classes?* Irodalom – Tanári Kincsestár, April 2004)

I say all this again, in a somewhat more direct way, during a discussion on the night of Shavuos, the festival of the giving of the Torah. Hmmm, yes, I know, my audience are Jewish, in this case it is quite certain, because if the Jews are those who consider themselves Jewish, then they are Jewish, that's why they are here. It's 1 a.m., I feel good, they're listening and talking – they're better than the teachers.

Someone said on TV that "Jew" is a different word – it differs from words like "socks" or "fountain". I feel that it is so different that I lose my courage: I was afraid of putting this down, of stating that my listeners were Jews.

Although I always ask children: tell me, who is a Jew? Or, who is Jewish? Who do we refer to by that name? And they are always silent. So I ask them how it was decided during the Second World War. And then they reply, shyly, on the basis of religion and race.

This is it. How did they did decide at which times? Laws defining the Jews, these were new. And what does "on the basis of race" mean? That there are Jews, and black people, and Gypsies… How can they be recognized? Well, their beard... And women? And children? The people who do not have beards? Well, yes. And what does race mean? Silence. If there were real racial differences, we would not be able to procreate, as our genes would be different to such an extent. Silence.

Based on my own system of arguments, I must raise the question about those who are sitting here now: on what basis do they call themselves Jews? If they are not religious? Because of the past, their families' past?

For a long time, whenever I was asked why I dealt with this theme (or in a more prickly fashion: Why do you deal with this theme exactly?), I answered, understanding the main point of the question (Are you Jewish?), that I did not really know, it wasn't to do with my family, it's just that I thought it was very important. And with this I answered their unspoken question too: No, I am not Jewish.

But what does being concerned mean? Can it be that the only ones concerned are the ones who suffered or died in concentration camps, or hid at home in cellars, or at friends' apartments, or with false identification papers?

We are watching TV with my husband. *The Eyes of the Holocaust.* I have already seen it once. I did not cry then. I didn't like the parts meant for effect, the blood like dripping red wax, the healthy children's faces. Now I am watching it, and I don't want to cry, but I am weeping, howling. An old man tells that they were marching in the street, they were taken away, and there was no compassion on people's faces. There were people who laughed at them. My husband says: they were our ancestors, laughing there.

And so I understood. Everyone is concerned, each family. My grandparents were young adults at the time. What did they do? Did they laugh? There are stories about grandparents in every family. Why is it that I don't hear stories about how they hid people?

I ask my mother. I am surprised by the fact that she answers from a child's point of view, when she is fifty. She says yes, her parents did hide Jews, she remembers that. But Mom, how could you remember? Vera and her family came one night, and Zsuzsi was afraid of everything, even in America... But Mom, you were born in 1954... Oh, yes. Well, perhaps it was in 1956. But they were Jews, that's why they left, you know, Péter and Zsuzsi went to America, and Zsuzsi went to London with her family. I know.

I have a dim knowledge of something else, too, as far as my family is concerned. I begin to search, and I find a yellow sheet of paper, with a typewritten text:

Statement

We, the undersigned hereby declare that we know Mrs. Laszló Göbl, formerly Mrs. Máté Csák née Erzsébet Radics personally.

She used to work as a Christian nurse at the children's ward at 6 Zoltán Street, Budapest, 5th district, as an employee of the Red Cross, during the assault on the Capital. From October 1944, 240 Jewish children and 60 Jewish adults stayed in this institution permanently.

We testify, as eyewitnesses, that Mrs. László Göbl was brutally and severely attacked on 31st December 1944, during the reign of the pestilent Hungarian Nazi regime, while she dutifully carried out her profession, because she defended those she had taken care of, and refused to hand them over to the Nazi murderers.

During the assault by the Nazis, her fiancé, János Váczi, was shot dead in front of her, and she was hit so hard in the head with the butt of a rifle that her skull was smashed, and she had to be operated on and treated by doctors for more than 6 months.

As far as we know, she is still not healthy: she needs constant medical attention.

Budapest, 6th August 1946

Another signature, that of a police master sergeant certifies that the above signatures are genuine, but I cannot decipher either his name, nor the names of the others.

One has to see the whole paper, its impossible spelling, the arabesque, inked signatures, the stamp, the sixty year old fold marks.

Mrs. László Göbl née Erzsébet Radics is the sister of my great-grandmother. My grandmother's aunt.

So is it better now? Is it better, as far as my family is concerned? Perhaps it is better than to find out that "during the reign of the pestilent Hungarian Nazi regime" my ancestors were Nazis. It is better than that. But otherwise?

A friend of mine, who says she is half Jewish, told me she knew people who still judged others on the basis of the question: Would you hide them, or wouldn't you? And I got scared. Would I hide people or not? No family paper can prove that – one only knows in that situation.

So, to return to that late night discussion, someone remarks that it's not good if children only hear about the Jews in the context of the Holocaust. And another aim of mine comes to my mind. That the children should not think only of the Jews when hearing about the Holocaust. But I don't say this. Why?

An acquaintance of mine said that the Jews had appropriated the Holocaust. She/he surely is not thinking of the fact that Gypsies, homosexuals, people with physical and mental disabilities were also methodically killed in the concentration camps. She/he gave me a good piece of advice too. Be careful, people will think you are a Jew, too. Although it may be good for you, they stick together. Of course I understand that, it's no problem, they help their kind. I began to argue with her/him, but perhaps I was not forthright enough. Her/his stupidity made me sick.

When it turns out that I deal with Holocaust education, suddenly some doors open before me. Why? Because more and more people see that it's important? But I have been invited to places where they haven't even known me, just because a Jewish girl (a girl professing to be a Jew) recommended me. Why? Is this that oft mentioned "sticking together"? Why must I think about that?!

Another acquaintance congratulates me for "working myself into the subject so well". I get hurt. As it turns out, he/she meant it as an acknowledgment. Am I paranoid?

As for what people think of me... I have been many things: "Móni Molnár's gypsy-looking girlfriend" in primary school, an "Egyptian beauty" in high school. People sometimes ask me if I speak Hungarian. When I was a university student, I gave lessons to the daughter of someone famous, and she said she had known it about me immediately, that I was like that, too. I was like what? That I was Jewish. For a moment I imagined what would have happened if I hadn't objected. After all, it would be easier not to say no to a girl who does not eat because her grandfather starved in a concentration camp. Then I answered that I did not know of anyone in my family who was… Jewish. Just like that, with a little pause. I don't remember what her answer was.

As a matter of fact, I was a bit afraid. What if I was? Others can see it, but my family wanted to keep it secret…

"I was expecting that they would sob, like converted sinners, that after being cleansed and liberated by sobbing they would share the Jewish shame with me, somehow dissolving my secret, Jewish fear." (Gábor Németh: *Are You Jewish?*)

Is it possible that I was ashamed at that moment, lasting for half a second, because I am not Jewish? Is it possible that this is why being afraid stayed with me?

"Namely," he then said, "Uncle Aurél thinks that we are Jews."

Zsolti smiled at that. Ákos, who always reacted more intensely, shook with laughter.

"But that's crazy, Papa! Who told him such a stupid thing?"

"This isn't a stupid thing," his father said sternly. "He and I, all our family, are of Jewish origin." (István Örkény: *Ákos and Zsolt*)

I am sitting on a bus with a textbook on my lap, the best one on this subject: *Ways to the Holocaust, Stories about the Holocaust.* I hold a bag on the book, and I lay my hand on the bag. An older woman is sitting next to me; she leans forward, in an extremely indiscreet way, towards the book, and my lap. She reads the title. I am embarrassed, not because of the book but because of her indiscretion, as she is staring at my lap unwaveringly. I want to say something to break this awkward silence, so I say I am going to teach. – About this? she asks. Yes, I say to her, using my nonexistent neutral voice. – There are so many lies surrounding it, she replies, and I don't know how she means it, pro or contra. Yes, I say, waiting for her to continue. Of course she meant it "contra": and she begins to juggle with numbers. That there were not so many people. Only 300,000 Hungarian Jews died. And she finishes with a foolproof argument: "My Jewish friends told me that." Then she gets off at the next stop. If this can happen today in a bus, what do people say at home, when they are with their families, between the four walls?

I am on my way to teach about the Holocaust. I may tell them this story, if the group is conducive to that sort of thing. I am walking along Üllői Street. This is the second time, I am still a bit worried and excited. I have not decided whether I should bring the children's attention to the factory scenes they can see in a film composed of documentaries made in the thirties, where they can see how eyeglass frames and shoes were made on a production line, and the piles of eyeglasses and shoes they can see at the end of the exhibition, which stand for dead people, or whether I should let them discover these things for themselves. I am getting close to the Páva Street Holocaust Memorial Center. I am watching my steps.

"She directed our steps so that we ended up in front of the huge mirror in the hall. We stopped there. I was watching her, both of us, standing next to one another, reflected in the mirror. She didn't need much force, she turned my head with her palm resting on my nape, so that I could see only myself, from close up, so that she did not even have to point at me.

Well then watch him carefully, she said silently, there's a Jew for you, you can hate him, as much as you want.

Since then I am watching who I am. Since then I think about what I can state about others, and about ourselves. Since then, whenever I look into a mirror, it is not myself that I see, but the person who looks at someone in the mirror." (Péter Nádas: *Yearbook*)

Translation by Bea Sándor

Zsuzsa Tamás

Zsuzsa Tamás was born on March 8, 1978 in Budapest. She graduated from ELTE, but even before she completed her thesis she began teaching. Since then she's left the teaching profession twice already, on one occasion this was not of her own chosing. She publishes regularly in pedagogical and non-profit journals.

Anna Szász

WHAT DOES BEING JEWISH MEAN?

„I feel sorry for the Jews, but they are to blame for what happened. When Jesus was crucified, they foretold that the sins of the fathers would be visited on the children."

It was the autumn of 1945, or the spring of 1946. My form master in the Sze. Street Elementary School was a small, thin, gap-toothed woman who stood in front of the teacher's desk far away from me. If you stood next to her, you could feel the almost unbearable, foul smell coming from her mouth.

There were forty of us in the class, all of us girls, and four of us were Jewish. Between the four of us we'd lost four parents. Two of us lost our fathers, there was one girl whose parents remained alive, and Zseni D. was the one who became an orphan.

Zseni was born in Berlin, in September 1933. Her mother was a German Jew, and her father came from the extensive family of the B.s – also a Jewish family, several members of which were renowned scholars. Her parents weren't married in those chaotic years, that's why Zseni got her mother's family name. She was six months old when they fled to Hungary. As foreign citizens, they had to go regularly to the dreaded KEOKH (Central Alien Control Office). Her parents were interned several times, and once Zseni had to go with them too. Her father was drafted into the cruelest labor service company in 1942, and he was beaten to death by the guards that winter in Ukraine. Her mother was taken away in the summer of 1944. She had to report herself to the KEOKH again, and they never let her go. Gerda D., a thin, epileptic woman, doomed to be gassed, died in Auschwitz. Until October 1944 Zseni had an with her too, but then she was also deported. Zseni was left alone. I tape recorded the story of her survival in 1992.

Not long after the shortened school year we spent in the Sze. Street school (we had many breaks because of the cold as there was no coal), Zseni was adopted by a married couple, two doctors. Her foster mother insisted on changing her first name too. So Zseni D. became Zsuzsa L. Her foster father died early, and she had many quarrels with her foster mother, so she moved away from her, began to work at the age of 16, and supported herself, if living destitute can be called that. She tried to commit suicide in the early 1950s, she took a lot of pills, but her best friend found her and took her to the hospital. Then she soon married a (non-Jewish) musical clown, who was a little hunchbacked and much older than her, but whose human qualities and goodness made her forget his unbecoming appearance. Zsuzsa used her husband's family name: her friends thought of her as Zsuzsa B. (Which was not the same as her father's family name.) Her husband, whom I didn't know personally, was called Ali: that was his stage-name, and his family called him Ali, too. When I received a death-notice in the spring of 1994, saying that the widowed Mrs. Mihály B. had died at the age of 61, after a grave illness, it took a while until I realized who she was.

"Are you a Jewish girl?" A woman asked Zseni in the street, as she was fleeing from one place to another in November or December 1944.

"But you are not a Jew!" they tell me when they say Anti-semitic things and I declare myself.

They mean it as a compliment.

*

In the summer of 1944 the graduating students of a high school performed *Laodameia*, a dramatic poem by Mihály Babits. The performance was broadcasted by the radio. Mariann Csernus played Laodameia. This was her first role, her début. I still remember her voice, after almost sixty years, and these lines: „Oh, I am calling my hero back / if only for a moment..."

I check the last half line in the volume: „...and then death may come".

We had a terrible heatwave that summer. We slept naked under our sheets at night.

And we were still lucky: the seven us lived in the apartment of my aunt S., in four rooms. There was she, my cousin M., another cousin of mine P., my grandfather, and the three of us, my mother, my younger brother and me. It was in the middle of the summer that a tall, gentle, elderly man was sent to stay with us. He didn't bother us much. He moved into the room that used to be the maid's. He used the bathroom very early in the morning. One day he didn't come out. My mother told me that he had fallen asleep, he'd died. She and my grandfather tried to convince me to have a look at him: „A beautiful dead man." But I didn't want to. I didn't want to see him. I didn't want to look at death so closely. Even if it was beautiful.

*

How does a child living in an assimilated family find out that she is a Jew? We didn't keep the high holy days. Neither my parents, nor my grandfather attended the services. There were no objects in our home that would have revealed our being Jewish. Perhaps it happened during an excursion.

I was with my father, his friends and the children of my aunt E. We reached the top of a hill, and there were other children there, 7 and 8 year old boys, and they shouted something at us, which definitely contained the word JEWS. The memory stayed with us, like the memory of the pebbles they threw at us.

I think I wasn't afraid, I wasn't indignant, it's rather that I was surprised. As far as I remember the adults didn't explain anything after this incident. But slowly I began to suspect that something was wrong with us, for some reason we had to be afraid. From the whisperings of family members, their sudden silences. From the discussions on Sunday afternoons, which we spent with my grandfather's sister. A few expressions were dropped like: Czechoslovakia, refugees, KEOKH. Their emphases were telling. While the grown-ups were listening to the BBC silently, we children cowered under the huge, round family table, and I felt that something I could not name, a dark shadow was coming closer and closer.

By the time I began to go to school, I knew that we were Jews. The only thing I didn't know was what that meant. I was surprised when I found out that my grandfather knew how to read in Hebrew, he helped me recognize those difficult signs, read the printed lines from right to left. I thought that we, my grandfather, my mother's younger sister aunt E., who lived close to us, her husband and their children, whom we met almost every day, were all Jews. But I didn't think that about my mother's older sister, whose family lived far away from us, both socially and geographically. While her husband was alive, my aunt S. lived up on Rózsadomb, an elite part of the city, I wouldn't have thought that they were Jews too.

I was probably already a schoolgirl when I heard Hitler talk on the radio. That voice, his howling was menace itself. German was a second mother tongue to my parents, and I understood a lot, but I was not willing to learn it.

I saw the newsreel in the cinema: German soldiers were marching, wearing steel helmets. I could read well by the time an issue of the *Magyar Futár* (Hungarian Messenger) got into my hands, with a serialized novel, Lajos Dövényi Nagy's „He started from Tarnopol..." (now it's published as a book), with the caricature of a Jew as an illustration. A bowed figure, knock-kneed legs, a long, bent nose, puffy, protruding lips. It didn't touch me: my mother and her two sisters were famous for their beauty, my father was a handsome, attractive man with his Southern look, black hair and dark skin, and my grandfather, who was tall and thin, was good-looking even in his old age.

No, I didn't understand what the matter was with us.

It was as if I had inhaled with the air the *aufklärist* view of the world: the conviction that people are born to be equal.

So what does being Jewish mean?

I was in the third or fourth grade when I took my younger brother to a service on a Friday evening. My religion teacher, Arthur G., threw up his hands in astonishment when he caught sight of us: he took a white handkerchief out of his pocket, made four knots on its corners, and thus made a kippah to cover my brother's head.

I must be grateful to our teacher, Arthur G., that March 19th 1944 did not find me completely unprepared. This short, rounded man, who always wore a waistcoat under his jacket, and a watch-chain across his belly, was not a pleasant man. He grabbed the boys' earlocks and pulled them. He taunted me with my name. But he was the person who was probably frightened and shocked by the deep ignorance of this Leopoldstadt company, and he taught us not only about religion, how to read in Hebrew, and Jewish history, but also tried to instill at least some Jewish pride in us.

We were given a few pink booklets about Jewish heroes and martyrs from him. They contained stories written in a popular style. Daniel in the lion's den. The three Babylonian youths. Queen Esther. Judah the Maccabi.

And it was he who taught us Jewish songs. Once, perhaps during Purim festivities, we even sang in the Goldmark room.

His faith and Jewish pride did not help Arthur G. He too perished.

*

19 March 1944, a Sunday. The weather was uncertain, sometimes cloudy, sometimes sunny. Our phone rang at 11 a.m. My father answered it. He was standing there, holding the receiver in his left hand, twisting the corner of his handkerchief which he had pulled out of his pocket with his right hand. All of his handkerchiefs got tattered at their corners.

The conversation didn't last long. He put back the receiver and turned to my mother: „It was P." That is, my aunt E.'s husband. „Our friends have arrived."

He didn't say anything more. I still knew exactly what he meant. The Germans had come. I also knew the consequences of this.

I went into my room silently. I took out one of those pink booklets from the drawer of my desk. I don't remember which one it was, only that I began to read, and while reading, I decided that I would die as a proud martyr, with my head held high, without fear.

Later I didn't want to die any more. And I was afraid.

*

In February 1945 my cousin M. took out a vial of potassium cyanide from my mother's bag in my presence. It was two or three grams: a white, crystalline substance. We threw the vial into the toilet and then flushed it.

My mother told me later: this had been her reserve, kept as a solution in case there was no other choice left. She decided that she would do everything with us – until they put us in wagons. In the summer of 1944 she spent nights wondering which of us she should poison first if it came to that.

She had another kind of drug too. She took it sometime at the end of October or the beginning of November 1944, when my younger brother and I were in the Red Cross camp in Kolumbusz Street. She was in a Swiss protected house on the Újpest bank of the Danube with my grandfather, and since she had sent the family's common schutzpass to my father who was doing labor service somewhere in Transdanubia, she was left there without identification papers, knowing that the Hungarian Nazis could come at any time.

She got the schutzpass through Kató A.

As a child, I didn't fully understand or note the role people played. The thing itself, today symbolized by the name Auschwitz, or called the Holocaust, or Shoah, for this we had no language when it was all happening. Later it was signified by the year 1944 (I could never use the expression „vészkorszak" – the age of disaster, for some reason). But back then, it was all so impossible, so unbelievable, so incomprehensible, that it didn't seem important to observe mere details. I lived from day to day. I wanted to survive. I was not Anna Frank. I didn't even think of leaving a trace behind me.

I know from an accidental remark of my mother that Kató A., this beautiful, reddish-blonde woman, who was also Jewish, with two children and a wealthy husband, a friend of my aunt E. (and my mother also once hinted of a possible relationship between my father and Kató), was very brave after the German Nazis occupied Hungary. She began to make, that is, forge and distribute Swiss passports.

Or there was that other woman I knew as Magda Bese. She walked in the streets without fear all through 1944, transmitting messages among the members of our dispersed family, and she brought us food, too, until it was impossible to move around in the city when it was under siege. It was she who took us, my brother and me, to the camp on Kolumbusz Street. We could only get there, in November 1944, from near the Buda side of the blown up Margaret bridge all the way to Zugló, if we were not wearing the yellow star on our coats, and didn't carry any identification. This way at least we had the chance of pretending that we were Transylvanian refugees should anyone have ordered us to present our papers.

Magda Bese was a maid in the house where my aunt E. and her family lived, until they could. I only found out after the war that she was a Hungarian Jew from Slovakia, who had escaped to Hungary in 1938. When Tiso's men came for them, her husband, a rabbi, did not open the door until Magda had jumped out of the window. My mother told me this, and I can still picture this scene, just as I imagined it back then. I could see their house being approached by men wearing boots and carrying guns in the dark, and how inside in the darkened room the bearded man orders his wife brusquely: „Go! Jump!" I didn't ask my mother any more details: about how Magda had gotten to the border, about how she'd managed to come over, how she'd gotten forged identification papers, and neither did I ask Magda's real name.

The drug that my mother took then was not a deadly poison. She knew that she would wake up from the deep narcosis. Did she tell my grandfather? Did they call a doctor? Was it possible to call an ambulance for a Jewish woman living in a protected house in the autumn of 1944? She had some kind of a certificate stating that she had been treated by a doctor at a certain point. Later, when we were in the house under Spanish protection and the Hungarian Nazis held a raid, she bandaged her head, took out this certificate and lay down. We sat down next to her with my younger brother. They didn't take her. But those who had been taken out to Szent István Park from that house, were also let back in the evening. (Did anyone intervene? Wallenberg, or was it Giorgio Perlasca?)

She was never willing to say who gave her the poison: she evaded the answer by saying *one has friends*. She didn't talk much about poisoning herself either, only that she was already conscious when Laci P., my father's close friend appeared. He was frightened by my mother's condition, ran away, and later came back with a Spanish protection letter and a referral to the house under Spanish protection for my mother and her two children.

*

The man wearing a leather coat, boots and a Hungarian Nazi armband turned up in the house under Swiss protection on the bank of the Danube which was our temporary home early in the morning to take my mother and my grandfather away. Just one day after my mother and aunt E. had come for us into the Kolumbusz Street Camp. They left in an SS truck, with two young SS soldiers sitting up front.

This (ascribed to my aunt E. in the family legends) was not an every day deed. It was told to me more than 50 years later by my niece, R., the daughter of my mother's younger brother, who is six years younger than me, and was there in the same camp with us. *Two old women, old enough to be grandmothers, try to put their past together from mosaics.*

And I lost my temper, as if it had happened yesterday. I know that my reactions were infantile and grotesque, but I felt that my mother had been pushed into the background, elbowed out of the story, and that it was unfair.

No! My mother and aunt E. left together on that day. It didn't matter that their relationship was ambivalent in more peaceful times. They were sisters, and they were naturally allied. They had many things in common. They resembled each other. Both of them were determined, strong-minded and self-confident. They were both fast when a decision or action was needed. Sometimes they were impatient. Both of them had, because of their upbringing, a basic honesty and decency in them, and they knew their duties. When it was about their kids, they crossed the city under Nazi occupation not caring about their own security.

Did they have a definite plan, an idea? I never managed to find out even if they did. The stories from that time are all short, concise. Those who told them did not care about details, they did not consider them significant, or they assumed that we, who listened to them, were well informed, and didn't need detailed explanations. We all knew, after all, how risky it was to do something seemingly so simple, *like leaving together on that day*.

Was it an accident that they met the two young SS soldiers in the small cigar store in Sz. Street where they happened to strike up a conversation? They talked about old times before the war. *Perhaps* the two boys enjoyed the fact that they could talk to someone in their mother tongue. *Perhaps* they were also fed up with the war. *Perhaps* they were tough guys, risking their lives for two Jewish women who were strangers to them, and for five Jewish children. Without expecting anything much in return. For peanuts – or rather a bit of tobacco: for two cartons of cigarettes in fact. But all this is *perhaps*. Anyway, they made their deal. My mother and aunt E. sat in the truck, next to the two nameless, and for us forever unknown young SS soldiers, and not much later they found us in that huge, chaotic camp working under the protection of the International Red Cross, where whenever we left the brick building in which we slept on a huge table, I always held my brother's hand, lest I should lose him. They appeared, unexpectedly, and began snapping out orders, the way they used to, telling us to get our things immediately, and a few minutes later all five of us – aunt E.'s children, me and my younger brother, and R., who was 5 years old at that time – were lying on our bellies in the truck.

There was nothing really scary about that man. He was neither attractive nor frightening. He looked around with more curiosity than enmity, into that room which was still new to us. Then my mother and grandfather prepared another room for us. We, my younger brother and I, were still in bed.

„I'll come home, even if I have to swim across the Danube!" This was what my mother told us when she said goodbye.

This is another day I hardly remember – only a few frames. A cold kitchen, a sink, a woman I was trying to get closer to. Madga Bese appeared, and I told her to tell aunt E. that my mother and my grandfather had been taken away.

The see-saw of waiting, between hope and hopelessness.

And then only the utter darkness, the powerless despair.

And when there was only nothingness, complete apathy, then, at about half past nine in the evening, they both appeared. My mother and my grandfather came back.

They didn't have to swim across the Danube, but they had to cross the Chain bridge, which was still standing at that time, through the darkened city. My mother told me later that they had been taken to Buda, and as they were climbing up a hill (the Rózsadomb), my grandfather noted that the B.s used to live there: that is, my aunt S. and her family. My grandfather deduced from this that the Nazis wanted to find out where the B.'s were. When they reached their house in Mandula Street, the Nazis were indeed there, and they were sent into separate rooms and questioned. They were asked the whereabouts of my aunt S. and her children, about which they wouldn't have talked anyway, even if they'd known where they were. But they had no idea about any of that. After being questioned, they were locked up in different rooms. My mother was shut into a room on the first floor. She thought about escaping, climbing down into the garden… but how could she have left my grandfather there? But suddenly the Nazis let them both go. My mother asked them to provide her with some kind of a paper, something stating that they'd been there and released, but they weren't willing to do that. It was getting late, it was already dark. My mother told one of them: „Hold that lapel for me for a moment, please!" (This sentence, and that final „please" says a lot about her.) And there, in front of those Nazis, in the light of their flashlight, she unstitched the yellow star from my grandfather's and her own coat.

A few weeks later we went and left that house on the Újpest quayside. I never recognized it again – just as I never recognized the other buildings either.

In another life, in another era, I took my granddaughter, Eszter, to a private gymnastics class, in a studio, in a house on the bank of the Danube. I'd also gone there to do gymnastics for a few months. It was a late autumn or early winter morning, with the familiar fog floating on the river. As soon as I entered the gate, I suddenly noticed the blue majolica tiles decorating the entrance hall. I recognized it. *This* was that house.

Translation by Judy Weiszenberg Cohen

An avowal of Jewishness: a short, exact case history

I am crude and rough. As I get older there are things I like less and less, like… but I won't get into that, it's all the same now.

When I was young, I used every effort to win over everyone around me to an unknown party. That unknown, one-man party was – myelf. I'm still recruiting, no, that's not true, not any more, but I select carefully.

My childhood diseases: chicken-pox, German measles, whooping cough, mumps, measles, scarlet fever and an unidentified contagious illness. After the war I became itchy in the Sze Street Elementary School, literally. I'd been bitten by bed bugs, dozens of these reddish-brown parasites climbed out of my nightdress every night and I felt ashamed to confess it.

Anyway, I only admit my illnesses and faults in times of extreme necessity.

When I was 3, 4 and 5 years old, after my skull had been trephined, and my eardrum had been pierced several times, if I was awaken by a throbbing pain in my ears I was able, if not to bear it patiently, then at least to brace myself against it for hours on end. I could bear the fear, the strange visions. My enlarged thumb prints would vibrate on the wall opposite me, like narrowing and expanding black and white circles. I only had to silently call my mother to begin the process I so fully knew, with each of its minute details, at the end of which I could rid myself of the illness, but it was all invariably marked by pain and fear.

When I was born – in October 1933 in Budapest – I was sentenced to death, and the sentence came into force, but the carrying out of that sentence was postponed indefinitely, because of certain unforeseeable and accidental circumstances.

Katalin G. Kállay

AFTERWORD
Untold Stories by Jewish Women

This volume can be addressed by two ever-present questions of ever-present readers: 1. What is the significance of the case when an embarrassingly personal experience becomes a text? 2. How does the text, in turn, become a significant experience for the reader, often an embarrassingly personal experience?

Instead of focusing on the texts one by one, I will only pick out the title-story as an example – but I must admit that each and every writing in this book created a lasting experience, presenting me with old and new acquaintances and friends alike.

These texts describe experiences that are extremely hard to face for the authors, and the linguistic rendering helps them to place something that seems unplaceable in their life-stories. The words locate and tame the experience into stories: the *words* can be approached, befriended, learned and learned from.

The title story, for instance, evokes the taste of salted coffee through a practical joke that is out of taste – this way, the frustrating experience can be shared, it can become an example. The narrator's Israeli husband makes a bet with the guests arriving at their house: his wife, a survivor of the Holocaust, will not complain about getting salt instead of sugar in her coffee. Of course, he wins the bet – but the guests (together with the reader) are astonished to hear the wife's explanation: a warm drink from one's husband is always welcome, no matter what it tastes like...

Whether having had a taste of such a drink or not, we readers try to imagine the flavor, and likewise do we start tasting and drinking all the other words of this volume. It is a matter of taste what provides one with a foretaste of laughter or crying and what leaves a bad aftertaste in one's mouth. What truly matters is the primary contact between the words and our senses, only afterwards can we consider the associations created by the phrases.

These words: "salted coffee" may recall, for example, the "Black milk of daybreak" from Paul Celan's "Deathfugue" (translated by John Felstiner) or it may refer to whatever "bitter cup" for each of us is yet to come, but the salt can be connected with tears, like in the seder evening ceremony, it may evoke the purifying, disinfecting power of tears as well. A salted drink can be a potion of medicine, a remedy – and the image of salted liquid or water may be associated with blood or the sea, opening the story up to the scope of infinity. Among the motifs of the brief text, I found two Shakespearean parallels as well: at the end of *The Taming of theShrew,* Petrucchio and his friends similarly make a bet on their wives' obedience, and in *King Lear,* the broken King says the following words to Cordelia in a converting conversation: "If you have poison for me, I will drink it."

These associations were probably not intended by the author – therefore they may be taken "with a pinch of salt". As a reader, I have only recorded my own reflections, the way I found a place for this text among my readings, in my own life-story. Through the process of sensation and interpretation, the frustrating experience becomes personal.

But what if these memories are not only frustrating but torturing as well, if they are memories, in fact, of torture and pain? The book has a well-chosen subtitle: "Untold Stories by Jewish Women". At first glance, this seems to be a contradiction, since the stories are just now being told by the authors – but, going through the volume, one has to admit that there is something untold, something that cannot be told in each one of the stories. I think the choice of these texts is authentic because they can even share the absence with the reader. What the stories do not tell, marks a private region that is none of anybody else's business or matter of concern, still, there are a few simple objects and signs that convey enormous significance: a shoe, a photograph, a dress, an empty seashore... and so on. Let me call them meaningful markers of *absence* that seem to demand the presence and response of the reader. Whoever I may be, they make it possible for me to say (without frustration or embarrassment and trusting the aesthetic power of the words): "it matters, it's my concern".

APPENDIX I.

Édes Katám – my dear Kata,

Thanks for the book, it touched me more deeply than any I have read in decades. I am simply overwhelmed by the amazing women and their tragic-jubilant stories. I don't have a single friend or acquaintance, nor a surviving family member, whose background resembles my own so well. If I were younger and more mobile, I'd fly to Budapest to get to know them.

Congratulations on a significant accomplishment, you created a historical and literary Hungarian-Jewish classic that I hope will appear in other languages as well.

Judith Magyar Isaacson

Author of *Seed of Sarah, Memoirs of a Survivor*

APPENDIX II.

Dear Katalin Pécsi,
a hearty congratulation to this exceptionally welcome event – the birth of a new book about the hitherto Salty Coffee – *Untold Stories by Jewish Women.*

I am grateful for the invitation to participate from Toronto, thousands of kilometers away.

I am far – yet – I feel very close for we are treading on common grounds.

Advocating for women, voicing their Holocaust experiences is very dear to me for many years as editor of the web site: *Women and the Holocaust.*

To appreciate how precious this moment is we need to look back for context and remembrance. Last Monday was March 19, the 63rd anniversary of the beginning of our catastrophe and also the origin of many of the stories in this new book.

On that day, Karl Adolf Eichmann and his few hundred SS henchmen marched into Hungary as occupiers and with the enthusiastic, eager help of their Hungarian counterparts, the Sztójai government, the dreaded *Csendőrök* (gendarmes) and later on the *Nyilasok (*"Arrowcross" Hungarian Nazis) plus a "few others"- together they ushered in the annihilation of the vast majority of Hungarian Jewish women, children and men.

There are countless voices and stories we will never hear for they "morphed" into small particles of ashes scattered in the stratosphere or buried in unknown graves beyond our reach.

Those of us who came back struggled for years with survival and hoped that just being alive will bring closure – keeping the pain private and mute. But, as Charlotte Delbo said in her autobiographical book, *Auschwitz and After*: "I'm imprisoned in memories and repetitions."

In the long run there was no closure and the past continues to occupy the present – the force of our memories – often inherited by our children too – overrides other events.

Women survivors, living abroad, in increasing numbers abandoned the shield of silence a long time ago and recorded their experiences either for their families and/or for posterity. These stories shed an importantly different light on how women experienced the death and concentration camps, the struggle for survival and the aftermath, re-integrating into, often unwelcoming, societies.

While the Internet connected us earlier, in 2005 Katalin and I met in person in Budapest and she invited me to one of the, by now famous, evenings – where Hungarian Jewish women survivors were invited to tell their stories… and the rest is history. This newly published book testifies to the importance of witnessing while many of us are alive and able to do so. We owe it to those too who were silenced forever.

I wish the book, and the message it brings, in Hungarian and in English, great success and I urge all of you present to prevail with friends and acquaintances to keep on telling their stories – now, with global anti-Semitism and Holocaust denial on the rise – it is more important than ever.

Judy Weiszenberg Cohen,
formerly of Debrecen
survivor of Auschwitz-Birkenau,
Bergen Belsen,
slave-labour camp in Aschersleben
and a death march.

APPENDIX III.

Our voice

On the occasion of the *"Untold Stories"* publishing, I am sending from the far away Jerusalem my enthusiastic hooray.

These stories tell us about being a double-minority: both Jewish and women. They had been not only *Untold Stories*, but also silenced ones. Until now. Their authors had been missing not only from story-telling, but also from history. Until now. They had been dumb and had no voice. Until now.

The official voice of Collective Memory is history. History is also constructed of stories, although conservative historians distinguish and separate literature from themselves. But the decision what has to be included in history is a political question. The stories of minorities and marginalized groups are rejected from history, their voices muted. There is an ongoing latent fight between the hegemony and the margins about defining the inclusion's borders. Sometimes the minorities demand, sometimes they give up their space and voice – depending on their power.

According to Shoshana Felman, the Jewish psychoanalyst and social philosopher, the border-line between story and history is unacceptable, because *"the story tells about something that happened, and that something happened is history"*. The story "tells" about something, id est. – it has voice.

In the untold Jewish women's stories our voice is telling what happened to us. Telling the stories, printing and publishing them are a declaration: we are here, we are part of humanity, what we tell is considered, because our stories are indispensable bricks in the Collective Memory's construction. We have our own voice.

The initiative of *"Esther's Bag"*, the Jewish women's group – the collection of the stories, the publication and publishing them in this book – is our megaphone.

Hooray, hooray!

Katalin Katz,
The Hebrew University of Jerusalem